A Practical Guide to
Takeovers and Mergers

A Practical Guide to Takeovers and Mergers

JOAN BINGLEY

ICSA Publishing
*The Official Publishing Company of
The Institute of Chartered Secretaries and
Administrators*

First published 1996 by
ICSA Publishing Limited
Campus 400, Maylands Avenue
Hemel Hempstead
Hertfordshire, HP2 7EZ

Typeset in 10/12pt Times
by Hands Fotoset, Leicester

Printed and bound in Great Britain by
Hartnolls Limited, Bodmin, Cornwall

British Library Cataloguing in Publication Data

A catalogue record for this book is available from
the British Library

ISBN 1-872860-90-7

1 2 3 4 5   00 99 98 97 96

Contents

Contents

Contents

Contents

Preface

Takeovers are a rollercoaster which can make some physically sick and others exhilarated by the ride. On a more mundane level they are an extraordinary mixture of broad, long-term strategy and masses of technical details. For those who only occasionally have to handle major corporate events involving Stock Exchange circulars and advisers as well as students who want to understand the company's point of view this is the ultimate practical guide to what happens in the course of a takeover. I aim to provide the background knowledge that will give you the confidence to get the best value from your advisers and reference books. My aim in this book is to give a step by step guide which shows just how much is involved in a decision that should never be taken lightly.

My first takeover was a somewhat baffling experience where my colleagues and I dealt with advisers who spoke an unknown jargon and who would suddenly demand information without warning. By my tenth takeover in as many years, I had much of the information needed ready in advance and found myself on occasion offering reminders to the advisers. I had changed from being led to leading.

The book's main story-line follows a recommended bid by a listed company for another quoted company. Much of the work involved applies to any acquisition or sale of a company or business. Many of the matters covered apply to other events which require a circular to shareholders. Problems specific to hostile bids, flotations, overseas companies and buying in the company's shares are tackled too.

Advance planning is the key to cutting the hassle factor. Here I share with you lessons learned through two decades of practical experience. I point out ways of efficient working, explain the jargon and highlight possible traps and tripwires which are easily dealt with if planned for, but which can cause a major crisis if they are overlooked and then surface at an awkward time. All directors and officers need to be aware of the rules whose breach can cause serious embarrassment with the London Stock Exchange or Takeover Panel – not an experience to be recommended – and in the worst cases carry criminal sanctions!

The book provides a general background and practical guidance primarily for the company secretary in advance planning and dealing with the execution and the aftermath of any major corporate activity. It is intended as a guide and does not substitute for careful study of the current editions of the Yellow Book and the City Code and of the relevant legislation. Its application to specific situations will depend on the particular circumstances involved. It is strongly recommended that the reader seek proper and timely professional advice regarding any significant corporate activity. By reading this book it is hoped that you will be in a better position to ask the appropriate questions at the right time to achieve the most cost-effective result and to enjoy the fun and excitement.

Acknowledgements

My principal thanks go to my clients and employers whose active group development strategies have given me experience of a wide variety of deals and their problems, as well as a lot of fun along the way. Thanks are also due to my colleagues over the past two decades from whom I have learned and who provided support and companionship through some very fraught times. There are innumerable people from whom I have consciously or unconsciously learned much about the broad strategy and the fine details of takeovers and mergers both public and private. These include the many advisers who have worked both with me and for the other side, and many passing acquaintances. Special thanks are due to Professor Robert Jarvis and his colleagues at the Kingston Business School, Kingston University, and above all to Maureen Nolan, Information Centre Manager at the Institute of Chartered Secretaries and Administrators.

Extracts from 'The Listing Rules' which appear in this book have been reproduced with the kind permission of the Board of the International Stock Exchange of the United Kingdom and Republic of Ireland Ltd. Those readers who need to consult the *Rules* should refer to the 'Listing Rules', which is available from the Stock Exchange.

Extracts from *The City Code on Takeovers and Mergers* and from their annual report which appear in this book have been published with the kind permission of the Panel on Takeovers and Mergers. The extract from *The Company Secretary* which appears in this book has been published by kind permission of the Institute of Chartered Secretaries and Administrators. Extracts from surveys and research are published by kind permission of the National Association of Pension Funds Limited, Dr C. A. Mallin of Warwick Business School, University of Warwick, whose work was funded by the Research Board of ICAEW, and Stuart Manson, Andrew W. Stark and Hardy M. Thomas of the University of Essex, and the Chartered Association of Certified Accountants (ACCA) who funded and published Certified Research Report 35. This report is available from ACCA, PO Box 66, Glasgow G41 1BS. Finally, thanks are due to my husband Michael for minimal grumbling and much proof-reading.

CHAPTER 1

Planning a takeover

Introduction

Why set out to buy another company? Shelves of libraries have been filled with learned studies on the merits of takeovers and mergers and in attempting to ascertain whether or not such activity benefits the shareholders or society generally. Directors have more immediate concerns in reaching the decision to acquire rather than to grow organically. The shareholders' interests will be considered as the directors owe a duty of care to their shareholders; this duty is generally reinforced by the requirement that directors stand for election at the annual general meeting at fairly frequent intervals. Maybe a cash mountain is metaphorically burning a hole in the company's pocket. If a company has good cash reserves, the analysts and investors ask at every briefing when it is going to be used. If a company is short of funds or failing to generate internal growth, then there is a temptation to buy growth by issuing new shares in exchange for an extra slice of business.

Takeovers can purchase market share or new technology or good management in a desirable line of business or a distribution network or economies of scale or spread risks. Equally, owners can sell all these things. They also sell businesses which do not fit their future plans or sell a share of the future profits to gain the funds for expansion. Whether buying or selling, the change of control of a business needs a clear strategy, careful planning and expert advice. Many people only have the opportunity to buy or sell once or twice in a lifetime. In such cases it is vital to get matters right first time. There are many advisers to help, but advisers work best when the person instructing them knows what services to expect. This book is designed to give the occasional buyer or seller of a business enough background to have the confidence to demand first-class service of their advisers and to have some idea of what to expect as the deal unfolds.

Types of deal

My career has been in companies which did deals and which carried out a range of corporate activities needing Stock Exchange circulars. The main story-line is based on a full bid by a listed company for another listed company paid for at least partly in shares to be issued and listed. Most other forms of takeover, merger or issue of shares are simpler variants of that process. Thus in dealing with the main theme we shall also cover:

- a bid by a listed company for a private company;
- the purchase of a listed company by a private company;
- the purchase of a private company by another private company;
- the purchase by a company of a business;
- the purchase of a business by its management, usually with outside help, known as a management buy-out;
- the purchase of a business by its future management, known as a management buy-in;
- the sale of some or all of a business's future to release part or all of the owner's investment, that is, a flotation or placing;
- the issue of shares to provide funds for investment, a rights issue;
- the alteration of a company's share capital, usually to increase liquidity, a scrip or bonus issue;
- the purchase of a company's own shares.

Why buy?

For a company or an individual, it is often easier to finance the purchase of a going concern than to find a backer for a startup in a new business. This is not to suggest that it is easy to finance a purchase, just that the backer prefers sight of an existing track record with positive suggestions for improvement rather than a theoretical business plan fresh from the spreadsheet. Unless in a new and almost certainly high-risk field, acquisitions lead to faster growth than organic growth does. This applies whether the growth sought is in turnover, profits, geographic spread or product areas. In a business where customers are large and widely spread, acquisitions may enable you to service their branches throughout the country with economies of scale in order-taking, invoicing, credit control, inventory control and the often lucrative business of after-sales servicing. The increased scale also provides the chance to invest in even more sophisticated and efficient systems, for example bar coding, or just-in-time delivery. When Neil & Spencer, makers of laundry and dry cleaning machinery, bought D'Hooge, which made ironing and folding machines, in 1979, it was able to develop its marketing from one-off sales with an average invoice of £20,000 to package deals supplying complete laundry refurbishments with price tickets 20 times larger. Shipping and installation costs for overseas customers were immediately more cost-effective and after-sales service in the United Kingdom more profitable.

Finding the target

The initial strategic review identifying the need for an acquisition will provide the basic data to start the search. Many of the likely requirements will be found in your own or a closely related business area. Thus the most common method of finding an acquisition is by knowing a company or some of its people. This has advantages because its market is known and the company may offer fewer surprises when due diligence takes place than the completely unknown. On the other hand, a wider search process not only increases the number of candidates considered but also provides a useful learning curve. In working through this process with a chief executive to whom I was an adviser, we identified that acquisition did not fulfil the requirements of market and timescale that the strategy had set. Instead, we achieved the objectives by the opposite route of selling the business to a larger company in the right field.

Make sure that everyone knows that you are looking. Have you noticed how many press reports of companies' results include reference to the search for expansion by buying businesses in a particular area? If someone thinking of selling responds to such a mention, you are immediately in the stronger position to negotiate as they made the first approach. For small and medium-sized businesses third parties such as accountants, solicitors, company brokers, administrators and receivers are frequent sources of introductions. For larger businesses merchant banks are a fruitful source of contacts. In using intermediaries, establish that no legal completion means no finder's fee payable, and be prepared to negotiate on the level of the finder's fee if a successful deal is completed. Be clear in your requirements and make them widely known, but do not spend money on retainers.

Advertising is a surprisingly effective source of targets. Those who respond are seriously considering a sale. Again, you have the initiative in the early negotiations unlike a direct approach from you to the target. It may also reveal candidates which your industry knowledge had caused you to assume were not available. An advertisement in the *Financial Times* on Tuesdays or in *Acquisitions Monthly* can produce excellent results. To get results from this route:

- check the sector has sufficient targets in existence to use advertising rather than a head hunter-style approach;
- define your requirements;
- insert the names of two individuals and a telephone number;
- be there to receive the calls – your targets will not want to leave numbers nor to have return-calls at a time not of their choosing;
- do not use a box number;
- when replies come from advisers or venture capitalists get to the actual seller.

Other sources of contact are company directories, databases, trade press, exhibitions and advisers' lists. Desk research and various advice desks can be very useful when looking overseas. Advisers with a knowledge of the local culture and ways of doing business, especially those who can contrast the local ways with your own, are invaluable when bidding in an overseas market.

Making the approach

If the target is interested in selling or has made the first approach, the initial discussions are fairly straightforward. If the right target for you has not seriously considered selling, then a form of courtship may be necessary. A potential bidder should monitor developments in the target and its markets. Keep yourself well informed of changes which may affect the decision to sell or the market value, for example a change in management or in one of its competitors. Find opportunities to communicate and even to collaborate with the prospective target. Regular contact is vital in building trust and mutual understanding. As with any activity, keep paying attention to the matter, prepare thoroughly for meetings and telephone conversations, and set a timetable to monitor activity and to make sure that interest is maintained.

Before starting the negotiation, try to understand the prospective vendor's position. The various members of its board and senior staff will have different motivations and concerns as matters develop. Spend time imagining yourself in each of their shoes. If the target is a private company, any data available on the shareholders and on their personal and tax positions will help you to understand which aspects may be deal-breakers and which could make it happen. Role-playing before a critical meeting may help you to understand their negotiating stance and to clarify your own. Rehearsals inform and enhance the real performance.

The best and lasting deals are structured to suit both parties. They progress at a smart though not breakneck pace and in an atmosphere of mutual respect. If the agreement cannot be arranged to achieve your key objectives, walk away. The worst drain on a company is the pet project of the managing director that no one stopped before it was too late and where it takes a crisis to cut the ensuing losses.

Why sell?

A vendor will usually have a financial reason for selling. This can be a receiver or manager/shareholders trying to save something before circumstances force a closure or receivership. The sale of Dillons to Thorn EMI is an example. At the other extreme, new capital may be needed for expansion or development. The vendor may seek to maximise the value of the company over time and to share its future success with those whose investment make the growth possible. For such vendors, a placing or flotation may well be the chosen vehicle.

There may be good commercial reasons for a sale. A change in the direction of a group, a decision to concentrate on the core business or a desire to reduce gearing in changing markets are all valid reasons to put a subsidiary or division up for sale. A family company may lack succession, an owner-manager may be old or ill, or an unexpected offer or advertisement may open the mind to attractive alternative investments.

In a public company the offer may be unsought and unwelcome to the management. In a hostile bid there may be a good and reasonable defence of the status quo. Even then, major changes often follow. One wonders to what extent the mere existence of the Hanson stake led to the separation of ICI and Zeneca. In many bids, before matters become public the offer is improved to the point where the board is advised that the offer is in the shareholders' best interests and that the directors have no alternative but to make that recommendation to their shareholders in order to fulfil their fiduciary duty.

In negotiations advance planning and role-playing help gain the maximum benefits to the vendor. Recognise your internal conflicts of interest and avoid airing them in front of the buyer. I was not present at one negotiation but helped to document the very successful purchase which resulted when the purchaser fielded one director (not always the same one) and one lawyer at each round-table meeting and the vendor had a team of six or more each time. By the simple technique of saying absolutely nothing the buyer achieved a bargain because the other side could not resist filling the silence with their internal strife.

Methods of acquisition

There are four main ways to structure a takeover transaction:

1. purchase by agreement with each shareholder;
2. purchases of blocks of shares by private arrangement or by market purchase;
3. public offer to all the shareholders of the offeree to acquire all or a proportion of their shareholdings;
4. scheme of arrangement under the Companies Act 1985, sections 425–427.

The first way is clearly only practicable for a target with a small number of shareholders. It is, however, the most common form of takeover. Many of the general considerations for preparation apply to this type of takeover. The documentation is covered in the early part of Chapter 8 and the problems of integration of the acquired business following a successful completion are similar in most cases.

The second method is generally only suitable to build up a substantial block of shares. This block can either be held on a long-term basis for strategic reasons or could form a platform from which to launch an offer for the remainder of the share capital. Long-term cross-shareholdings are an accepted way of cementing relationships with Japanese business partners and across southern Africa. Strategic shareholdings on a long-term basis are the most common and acceptable form of investment in much of mainland Europe. In Anglo-Saxon countries such a stake-building exercise is usually viewed as a predatory move. US and Australian regulators and the UK City Code lay down very strict rules governing such stake-building which must be adhered to in the jurisdictions where they apply. The City Code contains an entire section relating to SARs, as the rules governing substantial acquisitions of shares are commonly known. There are also disclosure requirements in the Companies Acts which apply to all UK companies, not only to those to which the City Code applies.

The public offer by way of documents by or for a UK-based company is the main topic of this book. Stock markets throughout the world regulate public offers, and expert advice should always be sought in carrying out such a transaction.

In some complicated cases the schemes of arrangement provisions of the Companies Acts may be useful. Examples include setting up a new holding company to take over two companies with the intention of then merging their businesses and the purchase of the target's business where more than 75 per cent of its shareholders are known to approve the proposals but more than 10 per cent are against. These procedures are complex. They require the approval of the court and of resolutions passed by a 75 per cent majority of the members or creditors of each company concerned. However, they can enable a form of restructuring which would not otherwise be possible to be achieved.

Where it is not necessary for the offeree company to continue to have a separate existence as a legal entity after the takeover is complete, the merger of two businesses may be effected by the liquidation of the offeree company whose liquidator then sells the assets and business of the company to the purchasing company in exchange for shares which are distributed to the offeree's shareholders. This route has attractions where the target has a weak balance sheet. In such a case the new shares can be issued partly paid and the further calls on those shares can provide fresh working capital for the merged business. In all cases the early involvement of legal and taxation advisers is strongly recommended. Corporate finance advisers may be able to offer creative solutions to overcome seemingly intractable difficulties in the way of mergers if they are offered the opportunity to contribute at an early point in or before the start of negotiations.

Flotation

The term 'flotation' is commonly used to describe the process of raising cash at the same time as seeking a listing for the shares of the company. It is also used when a quotation is sought on the Alternative Investment Market or in special situations. The Financial Services Act 1986 regulates any invitation to potential investors which is publicly advertised. Thus it applies to any company which seeks to raise cash from the general public whether or not a formal market is provided for the shares. Examples of companies with no formal market for their shares are football clubs and local independent radio stations.

Securities will be admitted to the Stock Exchange listing only if the Stock Exchange is satisfied that the applicant is suitable and that it is appropriate for those securities to be publicly held and traded. They should be brought to the market in a way that is suitable for their nature and number, and that will facilitate an open and efficient market for trading in those securities. For many prospective applicants, especially with low capitalisation or in a high-risk business, the Alternative Investment Market may prove to be a more appropriate and less onerous form of quotation than a full listing.

It has been a common practice for a company which wanted a listing to seek to reverse into a listed shell. Such a deal is legally structured as a takeover by the listed company of the company which wants a listing. This approach needs very careful consideration. Under current conditions a straight flotation has much to recommend it. The shell company's shareholders and directors often have an inflated view of their worth and can make that route an expensive choice. It may, however, be worth considering if the shell has plenty of cash or if it has the right shareholder base already.

Special types of business

Special rules are applied by the Stock Exchange to applications for listing and transactions by certain types of company. The Yellow Book has individual chapters for overseas, property, mineral, scientific research-based companies, investment entities. Public sector issuers and Eurobonds are also subject to special rules.

Purchase of own shares

Under common law a limited company was prohibited from buying its own shares as that was effectively an unauthorised reduction of capital. The Companies Act 1985 ('the Act') introduced a statutory authority under which a company may purchase its own shares provided that it complies with the detailed rules in sections 142–150 of the Act. The following two chapters of the Act set out the provisions for financial assistance by a company for the purchase of its own shares and for the purchase of redeemable shares. The situation concerning redeemable shares is fairly straightforward. With careful reading of sections 159–181 of the Act and of the relevant Articles of Association the procedure to be followed can be identified and executed.

The provisions concerning financial assistance can catch the unwary. The procedures are somewhat convoluted, apply only to private companies and require getting all the directors together with a person authorised to attest a statutory declaration under section 156 of the Act. The biggest pitfall, however, is ensuring that a transaction which involves the giving of financial assistance for the purchase of a company's own shares is correctly identified in advance. This commonly arises when assets within the acquired company are to be sold to reduce borrowings incurred to make a takeover. Any purchase of shares should be reviewed to see whether it could be deemed to involve financial assistance. If so, then the company giving such assistance must be, or be capable of becoming, a private company and of carrying out the necessary procedures in sections 151–158 of the Act. Often in the acquisition of a group, several companies in the family tree will be affected. If the companies concerned cannot become private companies and follow the required procedures, then the deal must be restructured to avoid the giving of financial assistance.

The Act makes a distinction between 'market purchases' and 'off-market purchases'. For an off-market purchase there is a cumbersome procedure, which includes obtaining approval by a special resolution of the purchase contract itself before it is entered into. In the case of a market purchase, shareholder approval can be general in nature. Such authority must, however, specify:

- the maximum number of shares which may be purchased,
- the maximum and minimum price, and
- the date the authority expires which cannot be more than 18 months after passing the resolution.

Any company wishing to purchase its own shares needs to consider the tax and accounting consequences. A public company also needs to consider the impact of the insider dealing legislation and the Takeover Code. A listed company must also comply with the Yellow Book and consult the investor protection committees. In the case of a general authority to purchase a company's own shares, the investor protection committees (see Chapter 5) require a special resolution which must be renewed annually.

The Listing Rules reflect the principles of disclosure of information and equality of treatment. The specific requirements (which also cover the issue of warrants or options to subscribe for or to purchase equity shares) chiefly relate to the notification of purchases. The company must notify the Company Announcements Office without delay:

- of any decision by the board to submit a new proposal to shareholders for the company to be authorised to purchase its own shares;
- such notice must indicate whether the proposal relates to specific purchases or to a general authorisation to purchase (note: the renewal of an existing authority need not be notified);
- the outcome of the shareholders' meeting; and
- six copies of the relevant resolutions must be lodged;
- of any purchase under the authority including:

- the date of purchase,
- the number of equity shares purchased,
- the purchase price of each or the highest and lowest prices paid, and
- this must be notified at the latest by 8.30 am on the business day following the day of the dealing.

A circular seeking shareholders' authority for the purchase by the company of 15 per cent or more of its issued equity share capital must include certain specified data about the company, including a working capital statement and information on group prospects. Where 15 per cent or more is to be purchased within a 12-month period, it must be made either by tender or by partial offer to all shareholders. The working capital statement must be based on the assumption that the authority sought will be used in full at the maximum price allowed and this assumption must be stated. If the purchase is from a director, major shareholder or any other related party, then the circular is treated as a related party circular.

Where less than 15 per cent of the equity share capital is to be purchased within a 12-month period, this may be done through the market only if the price paid is not more than 5 per cent of the average of the market values for the ten business days before the purchase is made. As would be expected, purchases by a company of its own equity shares are prohibited at any time when a director of the company would be prohibited from dealing in its securities under the Model Code. If the company has in issue listed convertible securities convertible into or carrying a right to subscribe for equity shares of the class to be purchased, the approval of the convertible shareholders must be obtained at a separate class meeting. The prudent company secretary will ensure that the terms of any new convertible shares include approval of any regular renewal of an authority to purchase any securities of the company at the time of issue. This avoids any need to have a class meeting at the same time as the annual general meeting approving any such renewal.

Where the securities to be purchased are not equity shares – for example, debt securities, preference shares – then less strict notification and other requirements apply than for the purchase of equity shares.

CHAPTER 2

Getting in trim

We shall now review the tasks which should always be complete and up to date. In a perfect world they would be. In real life, business demands get in the way of perfection. Some records are needed for disclosure to a bidder, to interested parties or in relevant documentation. It is much easier to complete these jobs with care in a considered fashion at an early stage than to do so in a panic after an urgent demand from an adviser. When you have been asked for the square footage of the shop on Madison Avenue on Columbus Day, or the exact definition of the preference shares in Hong Kong at the start of the Chinese New Year, you learn to take defensive steps in advance.

Material contracts

If the transaction contemplated requires the publication of listing particulars, then it will be necessary to list in the documentation all material contracts entered into in the last two years and to have copies of the contracts available for inspection. So a quick review of the contracts entered into by group companies within the last two years for those of significance outside the ordinary course of business is needed. Many company secretaries keep a running schedule of significant and unusual contracts to facilitate the preparation of the directors' report in the annual accounts. Properly kept, this should identify the material contracts. Probably some of those listed will not be classed as material for this purpose and others may fall out under the exception that contracts entered into in the ordinary course of business need not be disclosed. With the list of contracts it is usually not difficult to locate the contracts themselves and prepare copies.

If there is no running list, or if it is suspect, a little more thought is required. If the assistant secretary responsible for maintaining the list left during the past two years and there was a gap before the replacement arrived, extra enquiry for items which may not have been noted is a wise precaution. For such a search, the main board minute book is a good starting point as most material contracts will fall into the class of matters for which decisions are reserved to the board. If the group has proper reporting procedures in place even where such matters are delegated, there should be a mechanism in place for reporting to the board any transactions which are deemed material in the context of information to shareholders.

The task is most difficult in a flotation. In such a case, during the early part of the two-year period the disciplines and procedures common in listed companies may well not have been in place. Also at a time of startup or major change, material contracts are more likely to be entered into. Sale and purchase agreements, agreements with venture capitalists or financiers, property purchases and other significant transactions are often entered into in the run-up to a flotation or a management buy-out.

There is no clear-cut definition of a material contract. However, they are usually readily recognisable. Over the years my initial lists have usually included a few which it is later decided are not significant enough to include, but it is rare to find at a late stage that a major material contract has been overlooked. It is important to bear in mind that the exemption relates to contracts in the *ordinary* course of business. There are contracts of significance to the company's business entered into in the course of that business but not in the ordinary course thereof. A review of contracts still in force though over two years old is needed. Major suppliers or customers or fundamental contracts for patents may be caught by the definitions in Chapter 6 of the Yellow Book in this way. It is, of course, also possible that a contract entered into within the last two years may not need to be disclosed if there are no longer any active provisions. The materiality test has to be determined at the date of the listing particulars.

One point to watch with regard to timing is the material contract entered into on a separate matter during the course of preparation of the documentation. Legal advice may be needed to balance the requirements of disclosure and confidentiality. Examples would include joint venture agreements to bid for a radio franchise or, in 1994, for the operator's licence for the National Lottery. In any such case it is good practice to ensure that the attention of the board is drawn to the wording of the relevant disclosure at the meeting which approves the relevant document.

The Stock Exchange may allow all or part of a material contract to be withheld from public inspection. The request must:

- be in writing from the issuer, sponsor, listing agent or, where appropriate, other adviser;
- state why in the opinion of the issuer one or more of the grounds for omission applies;
- enclose a copy of the contract in question or, if the contract has not been reduced to writing, a memorandum giving full particulars of its terms; and
- include confirmation by the issuer that the contract is a material contract not in the ordinary course of business.

The grounds for the omission of any information which is applicable are that the Stock Exchange considers that:

- the information is of minor importance only and is not such as will influence assessment of the assets and liabilities, financial position, profits and losses and prospects of the issuer;
- disclosure would be contrary to the public interest; or
- disclosure would be seriously detrimental to the issuer and omission is not likely to mislead investors with regard to facts and circumstances, knowledge of which is essential for the assessment of the securities in question.

Clearly the earlier application can be made to the Stock Exchange the more flexibility is available.

It should also be noted at this stage that, where a material contract is not in the English language, a translation as well as a copy of the contract itself must be available for inspection. A translation of a summary may be acceptable if the Stock Exchange agrees. Again, early application for this dispensation is advisable. Arrangements for translations are more easily made at an early stage, thus avoiding a last-minute panic.

Section 212 register

Section 212 of the Companies Act 1985 ('the Act') allows any public company to require a person whom it has reasonable cause to believe to be interested in its share capital to confirm whether or not this is the case and to provide certain information. Many public companies routinely enquire of those listed on their share register as to the identities of their beneficial owners. The secretarial assistant running the register or the outside contractor doing so can provide valuable information about the ownership to those dealing with the investor relations for the company. Regular monitoring of the sales and purchases can also identify the stockbrokers active in the company's shares. This facility can also on occasion give warning of stake-building or of changes in the nature of the underlying investor base.

The register of enquiries and the responses which must be kept under section 213 of the Act is open to inspection by members and the public under section 219 of the Act. Copies must be provided at the cost laid down within ten days of a request on penalty of a daily default fine on the company and on every officer of it. At a time of takeover or other corporate activity the nature of the shareholder base is of considerable interest. When a bid is made, both your company's merchant bank and the bidder's will want to study copies of the register. So make sure that it is properly kept and will not make you blush.

I served one chairman with a strong merchant banking background who forbade the company to make section 212 enquiries. He believed that it was better to cultivate fund managers and not to have a register which would have to be disclosed to a possible bidder. In practice I found that a letter on similar lines to a section 212 enquiry, but omitting all reference to the Companies Act or to section 212, produced standard replies from most shareholders. One pension fund spotted that the Act had not been invoked and refused to answer my questions unless I phrased the letter 'properly'. One nominee acting for an offshore investor also refused. From previous experience I was aware that the nominee concerned only provided information under the threat of voting sanctions.

Major shareholders

Any listed company is familiar with the need to disclose shareholdings above a certain level through the Company Announcements Office. Many active investors only update these announcements monthly or when the level moves through a percentage point. Changes in the rules have reduced the number of ambiguities in the disclosure requirements and the number of disclosures needed. Nevertheless, some disclosures need a fair amount of work to ascertain exactly what is being disclosed, whether it is correct and if it is necessary. And major announcements in the press act as reminders to tardy investors to check how up to date the information is. For the annual report it is easy to let one's major shareholders know the date in advance and to ensure that the disclosure included therein is correct and current. Given the insider dealing rules, such cooperation is less easy to arrange. However a friendly spot-check or memory jogger in the form of a section 212 enquiry may do the trick with the known problem shareholders to avoid the embarrassment to both sides of including information which is wrong in the listing particulars.

The group's activities

Study Chapter 6 of the Listing Rules in the Yellow Book for the range of information which will be needed. Gather the information as soon as possible and in particular draft the paragraphs of the document about the group's activities. Then consider the information gathered from the point of view of an investor. Have you mentioned any exceptional factors? Are there any items which have been overlooked? They could be new and not yet on the checklist or summary from which the information was drawn. Or they may fall just below the 10 per cent level and yet be crucial to the purpose of the transaction. When Neil & Spencer started its solar heating business, we ordered 50 per cent more copies of the annual report so that the salesforce could prove that it was owned by a listed public limited company (PLC). Guess which new subsidiary was missed from the list of subsidiaries in that annual report, probably because it was new since last year? Yes, Spencer Solarise Limited.

In the case of a flotation where the company is new to almost all its investors, advance planning will pay off. Information on the company's activities, its history and its senior management should be presented in a readable form. In this case the help of a professional copywriter may be useful to turn the accurate facts into an attractive presentation to prospective investors.

Front cover

Documents will be used to persuade the target's shareholders to accept your bid and to ask your own shareholders to approve the proposal. There was a time when these documents had no separate covers but kept to a basic style in the interests of speed and economy. The timetable imposed by the bid process, especially where the City Code applies, does not permit a major design exercise such as that for an annual report or corporate brochure. None the less, shareholders receive high quality material by every post and a good cover will encourage the recipient to look inside at the contents.

A good cover will be simple but eye-catching. A colour available off the shelf, paper or card of the appropriate weight and limited colour printing should help to achieve the requirements of speed and economy. The style will reflect the house style of the bidder. The corporate logos of both bidder and target will usually be included. For an agreed bid, the use of the target's logo is generally taken for granted. However in a hostile bid a certain degree of care should be taken. When the target's logo is a trademark the legal position is clear-cut, if unhelpful. In other cases, the right to use the target's logo is uncertain. It has been known for the target of a hostile bid to sue for breach of copyright. The case was settled out of court and, as far as I know, there has been no definitive ruling on the right to use an unregistered logo in these circumstances. A case of bidder beware!

For a flotation document, the cover will be an important tool used to promote the company. In this case, advance planning is not only possible but also highly desirable. The cover of the flotation document is a major tool in building the company's image in the investor market and should also relate to its image in its own business market. The glossy cover should be carefully designed to fulfil both these marketing aims and to fit the company's style.

The cover must display prominently:

- the name of the company;
- the type of transaction, for example a placing; and
- the sponsor or issuing house.

Any photographs or maps used must be relevant to the company. For example, a picture of the Eurostar train would not be allowed for a company which supplied some of the cutlery used on board. Nothing on the cover, whether inside or out, may provide any information additional to that contained in the text of the document. This is because the cover will not be reproduced in newspaper advertisements nor on information services. Maps especially need careful review in this regard.

Directors' contracts

Directors' contracts are available for inspection by shareholders under section 318 of the Companies Act 1985 ('the Act'). They must also be available for inspection by the general public prior to general meetings as laid down in the Continuing Obligations in the Yellow Book. As directors' remuneration is seen by the press as a matter of public interest, it is not unusual for these rights of inspection to be exercised. Thus the company secretary will have a set of copies of directors' contracts readily available. It is however prudent to check that the file reflects the current salary and other conditions. It is also wise to remind the members of the remuneration committee of the disclosure requirements and timing if they meet during the bid period. If journalists inspect the contracts at any time, it is courteous to let the directors concerned know.

In the target company it is not unknown for changes to take place in the contracts of directors and senior staff when a change of ownership is likely. Such changes usually result in increased salaries and longer notice periods. These terms are, of course, subject to the restrictions contained in section 319 of the Act, which relate mainly to contracts for longer than five years. A prudent board will bear in mind that if the bid falls through, or if they remain on the board of the company when it becomes a subsidiary, then they will have to live with the consequent costs. This consideration should restrain over-generous impulses.

Defensive measures

The board of a quoted company should be constantly alert for the possibility of a hostile bid. It is important to keep the market's perception of the company and the external conditions under review. Awareness of the company's vulnerability to a hostile bid can be the best defence. Pre-emptive action taken well in advance is a much better protection than that taken after a bid announcement, which may be viewed with disfavour by the market or outlawed by the City Code. Efforts to keep shareholders and brokers informed about the company and to help them to understand its strategy will be appreciated. Such efforts will help to counteract any undervaluation of a company's shares as the market will be better informed about prospects and asset values. In addition, communication builds up human loyalty so that if the crunch comes, the shareholders will be more likely to wait to hear management's side of the story before selling. The neglected shareholders will often seize the first rise in the market on a bid rumour to sell shares with which they have become disenchanted.

Shareholder communication is a two-way process. Knowledge of your shareholder base helps you to target the right audience. Private shareholders as well as professional investors are influenced by financial journalists' articles and by stockbrokers' circulars. If a company has just one or two major funds as shareholders it can be vulnerable to a change in investment policy or a need for cash by a major shareholder. Cultivation with the help of advisers of the fund managers who are not yet investors can help to reduce the threat. A willingness to respond to widely voiced criticisms will also build support. The response may be by explanation rather than change. Following the publication of the Cadbury Report, executive chairmen were criticised for combining both roles. Some companies changed the board structure and separated the roles of chairman and chief executive. Others pointed to their track record and convinced their shareholders that the executive chairman was the right choice for that company in the current circumstances.

Signs of a possible bid include:

- a sudden, unexplained movement in the share price;
- underperformance in the share price relative to its sector;
- bid activity in the market and especially the sector concerned;
- a cash mountain for which plans are not known;
- changes in attitude by leading shareholders;
- changes in the company's markets or regulatory environment.

In such circumstances when a bid may be expected, the board should review the company's advisers. Are they of the right weight and experience for the likely task, and which of them are also advisers to a potential bidder and so might have a conflict of interest? Close liaison with the financial adviser, usually a merchant bank, is essential to the successful defence of a hostile bid. Many aspects of the City Code apply to the period when a bid may be expected and expert guidance is required to ensure the proper steps are taken. The adviser will also have the expertise to prepare a 'Defence Bible' to enable a prompt and appropriate response to an approach, a dawn raid or an actual bid.

The time of preparation is time well spent. Even if the bid does not arrive, the efforts to put oneself in the shareholders' place will be of lasting benefit to the company. Identifying and addressing the group's weaknesses is often of long-term benefit. The company stockbroker has an important role to play. They can aid the shareholder communication process and also provide market intelligence on opinions about the company, its possible predators and its competitors. When the Stock Exchange operated its trading floor such intelligence also covered trading activity in the company's shares. Increasing automation has restricted such information largely to the business transacted by the broker itself. However, when CREST is in operation the timelag between trade and registration will be greatly reduced and so we may see the registrars developing further their role as information providers.

CHAPTER 3

Getting fit to go

In this chapter we consider areas which, if ignored, can cause serious embarrassment with the Stock Exchange or Takeover Panel – not an experience to be recommended. In the worst cases, failure by directors, officers or those close to them to observe the rules can carry criminal sanctions.

Directors' interests

Keeping details of directors' interests and announcing all changes should be second nature in any well-run public company. Nevertheless mistakes are made and records get out of date by oversight. When any corporate activity is in progress, public interest in the company is at its height and all matters of public record are subject to close scrutiny. Circulars to shareholders and documents sent to other parties require declarations in detail of the directors' interests – often in much greater detail than the regular disclosures. So at the same time that you remind members of the board of the insider dealing and dissemination of price-sensitive information rules, take the opportunity to confirm the true position on their interests. Those known to have spouses and family trusts, beneficial or otherwise, should be checked carefully. Many quoted companies are now adopting a policy whereby the insider dealing rules require spouses, companies defined as connected persons within the relevant legislation, and administrators of family trusts to sign the insider dealing rules to which the director himself or herself is required to agree. This is no guarantee that events will not take place which give rise to investigations and unwelcome, high-profile publicity. The company is in a better position to defend itself whatever the actions of others if these procedures are in place and all dealings are properly authorised and documented.

Interests must include all forms of security of the company, those held by each of the parties defined by statute and others which it would be proper to disclose even though the legal position may be ambiguous. For example, a self-administered pension scheme for an individual director – much more common since the introduction of the earnings cap – may hold shares in the company even if the main group pension scheme has a policy which precludes self-investment. To avoid misunderstandings where such pension schemes invest in listed companies, it is worth considering choosing names for such schemes which are unrelated to the holding company's name and those of its main trading subsidiaries. This minimises the possibility of misleading rumours at a time of takeover fever. It also prevents puzzlement as to why a company of great substance is apparently making small investments in unrelated listed companies.

The most delicate situation arises when it is necessary to identify holdings by trusts and other arm's length arrangements in a possible target. Directors need a delicate touch to ascertain the current holdings of such bodies without arousing unnecessary interest in the reason for the question. On the other hand, there will be a requirement to disclose any directors' interests in a target company in bid documentation. It can provide the target company with a card in a negotiation if its company secretary can casually say at the right moment when assured that the bidder has no interest in the target, 'But is not Mrs Deborah Blank the wife of your chief executive?' When this is agreed, the secretary then discloses that the lady in question holds 1,000 shares in the target.

What of the director who bought shares in the target before being made aware of the possibility of the bid? A dealing in the previous few months is likely to be criticised by the press and others. Paragraph 5 of the Stock Exchange Model Code covers dealings in the securities of another listed company at any time when, by virtue of the position held, the director was in possession of unpublished, price-sensitive information about that company. The Model Code however does not require such dealings to be the subject of the prior clearance procedure applicable to dealings in the securities of the company itself. That requirement was deleted from the Model Code in Amendment No. 2 to the Yellow Book (July 1994) as the Stock Exchange considered that the matter was best left to the statutory provisions on insider dealing contained in the Criminal Justice Act 1993.

So how can a director, especially a non-executive director, be protected against incurring undeserved criticism by such a dealing? Or how can the company secretary help the directors to avoid such a trap by alerting them to the danger?

The ICSA Company Secretaries Panel has identified some possible approaches:

- issuing to all directors a 'stop list' of companies in whose shares they should not deal, being possible 'targets' for acquisition by the company (this approach requires the list to be treated as secret and highly sensitive by recipients);
- requiring, in the company's code for directors' dealings, all dealings in the securities of companies operating within certain business sectors to be

cleared in advance with the chairman or other nominated director; for this purpose reference could be made to the FT-Actuaries Industry Classification System (which is subdivided into economic groups, sectors and sub-sectors) – the aim would be to identify those areas of business which contain, e.g., possible competitors of the company or areas into which the company might diversify;

- requiring, in the company's code, all dealings in securities of companies (in whatever sector) to be cleared in advance with the chairman or other nominated director; this 'heavyweight' approach is often adopted in companies in the financial services sector; these companies often also require any permitted dealings to be made through the company's broking arm to give added control over dealings.

Dissemination of price-sensitive information

Any quoted public company will have its existing rules about the dissemination of price-sensitive information and the handling of public relations. At an early stage, review these in the light of high-profile corporate actions planned. The Stock Exchange guidance on the dissemination of price-sensitive information sets out a five-point programme for investor communications:

- the board is ultimately responsible for controlling and releasing price-sensitive information; it should have policies to assess whether or not information is price-sensitive and to control how such information is released;
- the policy should define who is responsible for talking to analysts, shareholders and the media;
- those responsible for communications should be aware of the policy, for example, on important trading periods and on whether or not to comment on market rumour;
- price-sensitive information must not be allowed to leak into the market;
- advisers should be consulted, particularly when deciding whether or not certain information is price-sensitive. If in doubt, make an announcement.

The legal definition of unpublished price-sensitive information is set out in the Criminal Justice Act 1993.

Insider dealing reminders

As each person is advised of the corporate activity in progress, they must be reminded that they now become insiders. They must also be reminded of the legal requirements to avoid dealing in the company's securities and those of the target or bidder when in possession of price-sensitive information, and the need to keep such information strictly confidential. However experienced the board member, executive or adviser concerned, the company should protect itself by making the insider status clear straight away and reminding those concerned of their responsibilities.

The process of making someone an insider should be a considered one. If the reactions of institutional shareholders to a proposed deal are to be tested, it is not safe to assume that the recipients are aware of the implications of possessing such information. Discussions can be held in general terms by the corporate broker with the institutional shareholders to discover whether they would wish to be made insiders in certain circumstances. Different institutions have different approaches. Some will never agree; others are prepared to be consulted even if it means a prohibition on dealing for a period. A record must always be kept of those people who possess inside information and at what date this information was given to them.

These records may be called in evidence in a number of circumstances. The company may wish to conduct an internal enquiry at some point. The Stock Exchange frequently asks for these details when checking significant share transactions in the period immediately preceding an announcement. When the Stock Exchange finds cause for concern as a result of its checks, the Department of Trade and Industry (*dti*) may conduct an investigation. Such an investigation remains in confidence unless a recommendation is made to prosecute for insider dealing, or a further leak reveals the investigation. In the first instance the case will be tried by the courts and the records called in evidence. In the latter instance the matter is tried in the press and no evidence would appear to be required.

Physical security

Everyone concerned must be aware of the need to keep their working papers, draft documents and computer disks containing sensitive information in a secure place. Papers should be locked away whenever an office is empty and should be turned face downwards whenever anyone comes in. Computer files should be password-protected and preferably kept on floppy disks which can be locked away securely and not held on the main file server. If so, make sure that back-up copies, also password-protected, are made regularly and stored securely at another site.

Before sending facsimile transmissions, adopt the habit of checking that someone can collect them immediately or that the destination number you have is for a private facsimile in a secure and manned office. This is particularly important for directors based in regional offices or non-executives based in other premises where there may be no control over who may read a facsimile unless its recipient is warned in advance. In particular – and most of all if defending a hostile bid – beware the casual enquirer by telephone or at the regular lunchtime pub whose apparently naive questions can elicit sensitive information on your business.

Although proof-reading is time-consuming and ideal for work between home and office, *do not do it on trains*. It is quite amazing what documents can easily be read in the next seat or across the aisle when commuting, particularly on the later evening rush hour trains.

However great the pressures, make sure that the right documents go in the right envelopes. I have been made an involuntary insider for a flotation which was nothing whatsoever to do with me, save that the client used the same corporate lawyers as my employer at that time!

A review of the physical premises needs to be carried out on a broad basis. Where will the centre of operations be? Be realistic and review the requirements rather than just assume that head office has got the facilities to cope. An existing board room and second meeting room may already have many of the features needed. Consider whether either room is suitable to use for presentations to outside bodies. If not, plan to organise space at an adviser's premises or other outside location. Any meeting rooms should have telephones, facsimile machines, overhead and slide projectors, screens, and suitable chairs and tables. These rooms and key executive offices should be 'swept' for listening devices and other 'bugs' from time to time. Really secure arrangements must be made for the custody of any tapes of telephone conversations. It would be even better if the board rooms and senior executive offices were on a different switchboard from normal business as the general switchboard may need to record telephone conversations routinely. Review the overall security of the building. Make sure that arrangements are made to cover security, reception and the switchboard for the long hours which will be worked. Staff awareness of the need for security is the best defence. The people in the postroom are much better placed to notice the observer in a parked car or the too interested passer-by than the preoccupied chief executive or the overworked company secretary.

When two major merchant banks found they were soon to face each other across a street in the City, one equipped its windows with blinds and the other promptly acquired net curtains. While the business diary columns joked about this, both choices of window dressing provided some essential privacy from prying eyes.

So review your formal company procedures for communications to avoid the risk of being misrepresented or mistakenly accused of providing price-sensitive information. It is also important to review the timetable and diaries for regular briefing meetings as their cancellation or avoidance could raise the very queries you are hoping to avoid. Once an announcement has been made, one's corporate advisers, usually the merchant bankers, will wish to be present at any meetings with other parties. However, before that is appropriate it is essential that the normal rule of always having more than one company representative present at meetings with analysts and others should be strictly enforced.

Contingency plans must also be laid, in consultation with the advisers, to deal with unexpected leaks and market movements. There comes a point when market activity and rumour reaches a pitch at which the 'no comment' answer is no longer appropriate. Strict security and preparation is the best defence to delay this point to match the official announcement of your plans.

Corporate communications

Review all your procedures. If possible, put this review in hand well in advance. However retiring the company is generally, major corporate activity and Stock Exchange circulars raise the temperature and excite public and press interest. Ensure that you have appropriate public relations personnel on board, whether in-house or outsourced. Previous experience here is vital as you must know how far you can trust them and to what extent your particular public relations person can keep a secret. Cultivate the MPs in the constituencies where your operations are located. MPs thrive on photo-opportunities and will appreciate and remember suitable occasions giving local media publicity. Know who the shop stewards are and brief them appropriately. Staff should always learn of corporate plans and important developments through line management channels; nevertheless, a good relationship with the shop stewards can help oil the wheels of internal communications and reduce the exaggerations of the rumour machine. When defending a hostile bid, especially when jobs are at risk, not only your own staff but also local branch and even national trades union leaders may be useful allies. Identify your more articulate senior management so that they can be briefed to talk to local radio, television and press and to the staff during the course of the bid.

During any high-profile activity, and most of all during a hostile bid, a credible company spokesperson is essential. This must be a company director who must have:

- a detailed knowledge of the business and its environment,
- presence,
- credibility,
- numeracy, and
- stamina for hard work in unfamiliar and stressful situations.

This person will be the chief spokesman or woman at endless rounds of meetings with:

- institutional shareholders,
- analysts,
- press, television, radio,
- government departments, and
- the company's own personnel.

Be realistic. The non-executive chairman who shines at an annual general meeting or the 'back-room' managing director with the details of the business at his fingertips may not necessarily be the best public persona. Each company must choose, brief and train the right director for this important role.

Where to find your directors

Any director who takes his or her responsibilities seriously will want to be party to major decisions requiring notification to or approval by the shareholders. The corporate events with which this book is concerned generally include the issue of circulars to shareholders subject to the London Stock Exchange Listing Rules. The Stock Exchange requires that the board of directors takes responsibility for the contents of any documents sent out. The most important document in this respect is the prospectus including the listing particulars which is essential when a new class of shares or a flotation is in question. There was a time when a director who was abroad for some time could appoint an alternate director as a stand-in or leave a general power of attorney with another person to act on his behalf. While these arrangements remain available they are not regarded as adequate where taking responsibility under the Listing Rules is required. Current requirements are that each director shall have read the listing particulars, taken responsibility for their contents and have signed a copy of the listing particulars doing so. Where this is physically difficult, the power of attorney may still be used, but it will be expected that the power of attorney contains detailed reference to the deal in question and that the director will have had the opportunity to study at least an early draft of the listing particulars.

It is therefore essential that the secretary knows the whereabouts of the directors of the company during the period when negotiations are taking place and documents are being issued. Certain matters may be delegated to committees but several board meetings will be necessary in addition to the schedule of regular meetings. There are occasions when a director cannot for good reason attend a board meeting. With modern communications it should be possible to have telephone attendance or at the least to brief the absent director in detail by telephone or, with proper safeguards for security, by facsimile. Responsible directors will always indicate when they are away for more than a few days so that they can be contacted if urgent matters arise. When push comes to shove, miracles can be worked by administrative staff but it is much less fraught if the information on location and contact points is available in advance.

There was a merchant banker who, after a hectic period, decided he was determined to enjoy his holiday without interruption. Let us call him Rodney. Rodney had a new girlfriend, Frances, and arranged a holiday in a villa in Tuscany with her. The day he left the office, his principal client contacted the bank about to do a major deal. Neither his secretary nor his parents knew where he was going, other than 'to Italy'. His colleagues knew that he had a new girlfriend but did not even know her name. The quick dial buttons on his telephone revealed that his squash partner knew that he had gone away with 'Frances', but neither the garage nor the squash club had any news of him. The next number was unmarked but was answered 'Frances's telephone'. Careful conversation elicited that Frances had gone away for a fortnight to Italy with someone called Rodney and that her mother might know where. A call to Frances's mother revealed that she did not know exactly where, but that she knew Frances usually booked her holidays through a travel agent in a certain parade of shops. Some more persuasive telephone calls elicited the telephone number of a villa in Tuscany. Thus, when Rodney and Frances arrived for their fortnight away from it all they were met by the maid with a message suggesting that he should ring his office in London urgently. How much time, effort and goodwill would have been saved if he had left a sealed envelope with a telephone number for use only in emergencies.

CHAPTER 4

Target in sight

At this stage, the board has decided on policy and knows which type of corporate activity is in question. If an acquisition is planned, a target has been identified, and preliminary investigations and, possibly, negotiations are underway.

Preliminary considerations

If an acquisition is proposed, consider whether to purchase the target company by buying the shares or to purchase the business and relevant assets. Purchasing assets has attractions as liabilities can be avoided and only the assets required and the staff needed taken on. However, the liability benefit to the purchaser has a matching disadvantage to the seller, who usually resists an assets sale. A company sale has the benefit that contracts with customers come with the company and no novations need be negotiated. There may be a saving on stamp duty – ½ per cent on shares compared with 1 per cent on assets. On the other hand, if the purchase is to be funded subsequently by the sale of assets from within the business acquired, then a purchase of assets is the simpler course. If a company is purchased and a loan related to the purchase is to be repaid from the proceeds of subsequent asset sales, the financial assistance legislation comes into play. This is set out in sections 151–158 of the Companies Act 1985. Provided that the company purchased is, or can be converted to, a private company, the company can seek authority to give financial assistance for the purchase of its own shares. However, the procedure takes some time and should be avoided where the outlook for the market value of the assets is uncertain.

In 1989–90 there were problems for both the purchasers and their bankers of property companies bought at the height of the property boom. By the time the purchases made in the excitement of the summer of 1989 had been completed and the necessary legal hoops jumped through, the property market had crashed and both the purchasers and their bankers faced a yawning void between the level of borrowings and the value of the assets against which they had been secured. If you have ever wondered why some banks have property company subsidiaries unrelated to their mainstream business, now you know.

Stock Exchange classifications

Where either party is a listed company or a subsidiary undertaking of a listed company then Chapters 10 and 11 of the Yellow Book covering transactions must be studied in the light of the proposals. Transactions of a revenue nature in the ordinary course of business are excluded from these requirements. The regulations for methods of bringing securities to listing to raise finance which do not involve an acquisition or disposal are set out in Chapter 4 of the Yellow Book. The level of documentation and of consultation with shareholders required varies with the size of the transaction relative to the listed company. Chapters 10 and 11 of the new Yellow Book are much easier to follow than their predecessor, section 6 of the old Yellow Book. The language and presentation are much simpler, and codification within the rules of many of the items, which were previously dealt with by custom and practice known only to the market professionals or else covered by commentary, has greatly simplified the use of these chapters.

The classifications in Chapter 10 are determined by comparing the size of the transaction with the size of the listed company using percentage ratios. There are five test ratios:

1. the asset test, where the net assets, the subject of the transaction, are divided by the net assets of the listed company concerned;
2. the profit test, where the profit attributable to the net assets, the subject of the transaction, are divided by the profits of the listed company concerned;
3. the consideration to asset test, where the consideration paid or payable is divided by the net assets of the listed company concerned (whether it is the acquirer or disposer);
4. the consideration to market capitalisation test, where the consideration paid or payable is divided by the aggregate market value of all the equity shares of the listed company concerned (whether it is the acquirer or disposer);
5. the gross capital test, where the gross capital of the company or business being acquired is divided by the gross capital of the listed company concerned. This percentage ratio applies only to the acquirer.

The Yellow Book sets out detailed requirements on the figures to be used in calculating the percentages and the procedure to be adopted when one of these calculations produces an anomalous result. Whenever the results are imprecise or where the application of the definitions is open to interpretation, the Stock Exchange should be consulted.

The size classifications in descending order are reverse takeovers, Super Class 1, Class 2 and Class 3 where the relevant ratios are respectively 100 per cent, 25 per cent, 5 per cent and below 5 per cent. In addition related party transactions, formerly known as Class 4 transactions, are dealt with in Chapter 11 of the Yellow Book.

Once the classification of the transaction has been ascertained, the Yellow Book is then studied to identify the degree of disclosure and advice to shareholders which is required. Where there is an obligation to publish indebtedness statements, working capital statements and/or listing particulars then advance planning to achieve the information needed should start as soon as possible.

The reverse takeover situation describes an acquisition by a listed company of a business where any percentage ratio is 100 per cent or more or which would result in a fundamental change in the business, the board or the voting control of the listed company. This can arise by a substantial shareholder disposing of shares, a person or body corporate acquiring control through an acquisition of shares, or by a change in the board of directors. It should be noted that a shareholder may achieve control even though it holds less than 50 per cent of the shares.

If a transaction is classified as a reverse takeover, then it must be announced to the Stock Exchange's Company Announcements Office, whereupon the Exchange will suspend the company's securities. The company must then prepare a Super Class 1 circular and listing particulars as though it were a new applicant, although the requirement for accounts history is modified. If the quoted company's shareholders approve the transaction and the transaction is completed, the existing listing will be cancelled and, if the company wishes to become listed again, it will be treated as a new applicant. If the transaction is not approved or if it is not completed, then the suspension of listing will be withdrawn provided that the company continues to satisfy the Stock Exchange Listing Rules in all other respects.

Super Class 1 transactions are those where any of the percentage ratios is 25 per cent or more. These require an announcement by the listed company, an explanatory circular to its shareholders and the prior approval of its shareholders in general meeting before proceeding with the transaction. In practice, contracts for such transactions are usually exchanged subject to such approval being obtained.

Class 2 transactions, where any percentage ratio is 5 per cent or more but each is less than 25 per cent, are considered of sufficient size to require an announcement. The company must notify the Stock Exchange's Company Announcements Office at the earliest opportunity to comply with the normal disclosure rules.

For Class 3 transactions, where all percentage ratios are less than 5 per cent, no announcement is required, unless the transaction involves an acquisition where all or part of the consideration is satisfied by issuing securities by a listed acquirer for which listing will be sought. In this case notification must be made to the Stock Exchange's Company Announcements Office without delay.

Until August 1995, there was a further classification known as Class 1 for listed companies, although it never applied to the Alternative Investment Market. Transactions where any percentage ratio was 15 per cent or more but each was less than 25 per cent required an explanatory circular to be despatched to all its shareholders within 28 days of the announcement.

Although no announcement is required in other cases, if any details of the transactions are made public, these details must also be notified to the Company Announcements Office. The notification must include:

- particulars of the transaction, including the name of any company or business, where relevant;
- either the value of the consideration and how this is being satisfied or the value of the net assets acquired or disposed of; and
- if a disposal, its effect on the company.

Following such a transaction, the company secretary must be vigilant to ensure that all public references to it are limited to the details officially released. It is important that those dealing with advertising and the trade press are aware of any restrictions. A further trap arises in the case of a transaction where agreement has been reached with the other party to keep the level of the consideration confidential. A typical auditor's checklist for the annual report includes the consideration as an item to be mentioned in relation to any acquisition or disposal mentioned in the directors' report. It is all too easy many months after the event to fill the ostensible gap. If the item is not in the original press release, or there was no press release, alarm bells should ring in your head and the files be consulted before any further disclosure is made.

If any of the percentage ratios changes during the course of a bid to such an extent that the classification is altered, then the Stock Exchange must be consulted. It must also be consulted where a transaction is sufficiently similar to other transactions completed within a 12-month period that the requirement to aggregate the transactions for the purpose of determining the classification may apply. Details of these requirements are set out in Chapter 10.

An indemnity of sufficient size may need to be treated as a Super Class 1 transaction. This is any agreement or arrangement with a party outside the listed company's group which is exceptional whereby the company agrees to discharge the other party's liabilities and under which the maximum liability (contingent or not) is either unlimited or equals or exceeds 25 per cent of the average of the company's profits over the last three financial years (treating losses as 'nil').

Related parties

Related parties are those who are or have been within the past 12 months directors, substantial shareholders or associates of either. It is important to note that 'directors' include directors of a subsidiary undertaking, holding company or fellow subsidiary of such holding company and 'shadow directors', as defined by section 741 of the Companies Act 1985. In a group with overseas subsidiaries not familiar with UK requirements, and especially with subsidiaries which are not wholly owned and whose directors may be shareholders of their companies, it is essential that the management to whom authority has been delegated are aware of the related party rules. It is usually sufficient to brief them to check with the head office company secretary before proceeding with any proposed transaction. In a group large enough for communication to be a problem, it is likely that most related party transactions will be exempted under the *de minimis* provisions. It is dangerous to rely on this probability. Schemes of delegated powers should always provide for reference to head office of any matters subject to the Continuing Obligations under the Listing Rules.

The definitions of the categories of person regarded as related parties should be checked in case of doubt as these rules have changed from time to time. Management buy-outs are almost always related party transactions although often within one of the Class definitions as well. Where the director of a subsidiary is to be granted options over shares in a joint venture company, then both the grant of the option and its later exercise are related party transactions. The resolution for approval in such a case is best drafted to cover both the approval of the grant and also its subsequent exercise. As non-executive directors increase in number, the possibilities of a company doing business with parties in which its directors have an interest also increase.

Chapter 11 of the Yellow Book deals with the requirements for a related party transaction. An announcement is required giving:

- details of the transaction;
- the name(s) of the related party(ies); and
- details of the nature and extent of the interest of the related party in the transaction.

A circular must be sent to shareholders containing the prescribed information. Shareholder approval is needed either before the transaction is entered into or thereafter, in which case the completion of the transaction must have been conditional on obtaining the approval. If the related party or their associates hold shares in the company, that party must take all reasonable steps to ensure that they abstain from voting on the resolution.

When the status of a party to a transaction changes to that of a related party during the course of a transaction, then the company must ensure that the relevant party abstains from voting on the resolution and a further circular must be despatched containing any information required for a related party transaction which was not included in the original circular. A change in an agreement, such as a novation, between a listed company or one of its subsidiaries and a related party is subject to the requirements even if at the time the original agreement was made that party was not a related party. This can easily arise where an acquisition is made on deferred terms, the vendor joins the buyer's board and the earn-out terms are later modified.

There are a limited number of exceptions to the usual requirements. Any such possible exception should be checked carefully against the current rules before taking advantage of the non-disclosures. They are:

- the company has no equity securities listed;
- the company is an overseas company with a listing in London;
- the transaction is an issue of new securities either:
  - as a rights issue, or
  - following rights, for example conversion rights, already approved by the shareholders in general meeting;
- the issue of shares or grant of an option under all employee share schemes;
- the grant of credit in the ordinary course of business on normal terms;
- the grant of an indemnity to or the maintenance of insurance for a director to the extent permitted by section 310 of the Companies Act 1985;
- an underwriting on normal terms;
- *de minimis*, that is where each of the percentage ratios referred to above is equal to or less than 0.25 per cent.

Where the *de minimis* rules do not apply but the transaction with the related party is one where each of the percentage ratios is less than 5 per cent and one or more exceeds 0.25 per cent, then instead of the usual related party requirements the company must, prior to completing the transaction:

- inform the Stock Exchange in writing of the details of the proposed transaction;
- provide written confirmation from an independent adviser acceptable to the Stock Exchange that the terms of the proposed transaction with the related party are fair and reasonable so far as the shareholders of the company are concerned; and
- undertake in writing to include details of the transaction in the company's next published annual accounts including:
  - the identity of the related party;
  - the value of the consideration;
  - all other relevant details of the transaction.

Transactions between the company and the same related party within a 12-month period must be aggregated before applying the percentage tests.

In considering whether or not a transaction is with a related party, one should have regard to section 320 of the Companies Act 1985 ('the Act'). This section covers substantial property transactions involving directors and those connected with them. Unlike the Yellow Book, section 320 does not cover a purchase from the director of a subsidiary. On the other hand, if the transaction involves both a subsidiary subject to the Act and a director of that subsidiary, then section 320 may apply to the subsidiary even if it does not catch the group holding company. Section 320 has the effect, *inter alia*, of prohibiting certain arrangements whereby a director of the holding company or its holding company or a connected person acquires assets from the company or where the company acquires assets from such a person. The absolute cash limits in section 320(2) are changed from time to time by Statutory Instrument and the current position should be checked as required. At the time of writing, if the price payable for an asset is not less than £2,000 but (subject to that) exceeds £100,000 or 10 per cent of the company's asset value, the arrangement must first be approved by a resolution of the members of the company and, in certain cases, its holding company. Careful reading of sections 320–322 and of any amendments thereto is recommended in those cases where it may be applicable.

Takeover rules

The Takeover Panel is the regulatory body which publishes and administers the City Code on Takeovers and Mergers. This code applies to *all* public companies as it is concerned with takeovers of any company where the shares are held by the public. Thus it applies to all public companies whether listed, quoted or not. It should be noted in relation to takeovers that it can also apply to private companies. It applies to:

- any public company, whether or not it is listed on the Stock Exchange, which is resident in the United Kingdom, the Channel Islands or the Isle of Man;
- any quoted public company which is resident in the Republic of Ireland.

It also applies to private companies (resident as above) when:

- their equity capital has been listed on the Stock Exchange at any time during the ten years prior to the relevant date; or
- dealings in their equity capital have been advertised in a newspaper on a regular basis for a continuous period of at least six months during the ten years prior to the relevant date; or
- their equity share capital has been subject to a marketing arrangement as described in section 163(2)(b) of the Companies Act 1985 at any time during the ten years prior to the relevant date, for example, their shares have been dealt in on the Unlisted Securities Market; or
- they have filed a prospectus for the issue of equity share capital at Companies House at any time during the ten years prior to the relevant date.

The Takeover Panel was set up in 1968 in response to concerns about unfair practices and abuse of power. The Code has gradually developed since 1968. Although only three rules have been added, the rule book is considerably thicker than the original because of the volume of notes setting out matters of practice and interpretation. The general principles of the Code should be understood. The spirit of the Code as well as its exact wording must be observed. During the planning stage of an acquisition, the major requirements of the Code should be reviewed and considered. As the Code is subject to revision from time to time, make sure that the copy in use is fully up to date. Its impact needs to be taken into consideration as it can sometimes restrict the freedom of action of those involved in offers. The extent to which the Code is likely to affect both the costs and the timetable of an offer should be appraised.

If a company is informed that it is the subject of a takeover bid, or is planning to make such a bid, then parts of the Code are immediately relevant and appropriate professional advice should be sought as soon as possible. In the period prior to the announcement of an offer, absolute secrecy must be maintained. The secretaries of the companies concerned will be responsible for making arrangements to make sure that this secrecy is achieved.

On one occasion we held a board meeting in a hotel room before the company's annual general meeting at the same hotel. Traffic was gridlocked because of a one-day rail strike. The chairman was late, having abandoned his car and chauffeur in the traffic and walked across Hyde Park to reach the meeting. Shortly after the board meeting started, a courier delivered a letter to the chairman. It contained an offer for the company. As secretary I was asked to make copies so each member of the board and the advisers present could read the proposals. The hotel staff were most upset that I refused to give the document to them to copy but insisted that I be escorted to the photocopier myself. Seeing the dingy state of the basement where the machine was located I could understand their reluctance, but I certainly could not risk letting the letter out of my sight – especially with shareholders already arriving on the premises for a general meeting.

Our merchant banker was already present; otherwise we should have been glad that he always travelled by motor-cycle. Later in the day I clung to my handbag as one does in a crowded shopping street knowing that it contained the copies of the letter collected at the end of the board meeting.

Under the Code, any offer should, in the first instance, be put forward to the board of the offeree company or to its advisers. In making such an approach, the identity of the offeror must be disclosed. The board of the offeree company must obtain competent independent advice on the offer and is entitled to be satisfied that the offeror is, or will be, in a position to implement the offer in full. In the case above, this assurance was certainly required as the bidder offering hundreds of millions of pounds for the company was a newly incorporated public limited company with a share capital of just £50,000, the minimum capital for a public limited company permitted by the Companies Acts. Rule 2 of the Code sets out in detail when an announcement is required.

The City Code applies to companies in what were once called the British Isles. Takeover regulations are much weaker in much of continental Europe. Whereas in the United Kingdom the bidder is required to treat all shareholders equally, in mainland Europe the bidder regularly acquires only as large a stake as it needs for control. The successful partial bidder buys capital cheaply leaving minority investors with few rights. This different balance of advantage and disadvantage should be borne in mind when investing in companies in mainland Europe.

Competition and monopolies

Another point to be reviewed in an acquisition or merger is the extent to which this will impact on the operation of the competitive market in which the companies concerned participate. A review of the market share expected to be held if the acquisition is successful should be conducted. If this level is likely to attract an enquiry by the Monopolies and Mergers Commission, or to impact on the levels permitted under European legislation, then the consequences need to be considered. Planning in this case needs to cover both the contingency of an enquiry being announced and the delay and extra cost if the possibility of an enquiry is canvassed. Parameters need to be identified to guide a decision on whether or not to abort a proposed acquisition if an enquiry is announced.

The principal UK legislation in this field is the Fair Trading Act 1973 (FTA). The merger provisions are administered on the ground by the Office of Fair Trading (OFT). The authority to refer a merger to the Monopolies and Mergers Commission (MMC) is vested in the Secretary of State for Trade and Industry, also known as the President of the Board of Trade.

The definition of 'merger' is widely drawn in the FTA, including not only the acquisition of an interest of 50 per cent or more of a business, but also the ability to influence or control its policy materially. The legislation applies when:

● two or more enterprises merge; and
● at least one of those enterprises was either carried on in the United Kingdom or was under the control of a UK body corporate; and either:
● the merger creates or adds to a market share of 25 per cent or more; or
● the value of the assets taken over worldwide exceeds £70 million (this figure is amended from time to time).

If in any doubt about whether or not the legislation applies to the transaction under consideration, then seek a confidential meeting with the OFT at the earliest possible stage. Like most regulators, they are pleased to give guidance in advance to identify possible problems and to avoid future ones. Newspapers are subject to special rules.

Where the tests are satisfied it is usual to seek prior clearance. This is strongly recommended where the market share resulting will be significantly in excess of 25 per cent, where significant public interest issues arise or where other parties are likely to request a referral. The parties approach the OFT with:

● details of the transaction;

- information on any possible effects on competition; and
- any public interest issues which should be considered.

The decision whether or not to refer a qualifying merger to the MMC is taken by the Secretary of State (the President of the Board of Trade) acting on the advice of the Director General of Fair Trading. The advice may recommend that if suitable undertakings are given by the companies concerned to remedy any possible adverse effects on competition, then a reference would not be required.

There are three routes to obtain merger clearance from the OFT:

1. Confidential guidance before any announcement is made, in which case:
    (a) guidance is non-binding on the Secretary of State,
    (b) it is strictly confidential to the parties concerned and their professional advisers,
    (c) only government departments are consulted,
    (d) the OFT may refuse to give guidance if competition issues mean that it should consult third parties,
    (e) up to three weeks should be allowed for a response,
    (f) when, or if, the proposal is made public, the application will be considered as a normal merger clearance application, and
    (g) merger control fees are payable when the application is determined by the Secretary of State.
2. Companies Act 1989 clearance procedure, introduced as a fast-track procedure, in which case:
    (a) the OFT has 20 business days (subject to two extensions) to raise objections to the merger proposals,
    (b) the merger must be completed within six months of approval being given,
    (c) merger control fees are payable at the time of the application,
    (d) the Official Merger Notice Form asks for details of the parties, a declaratory undertaking and answers to 16 standard questions on the merger proposals, their effect on competition and the barriers to entry onto the market concerned,
    (e) provided the information supplied was neither inadequate nor misleading, then the merger may usually proceed without risk of reference to the MMC if no action was taken within the prescribed time.
3. Regular merger clearance procedure, in which case:
    (a) the OFT are under no statutory duty to announce their decision within any predetermined period, although guidelines require a response within 45 working days,
    (b) results are usually available within a month,
    (c) no merger control fees are payable until the merger is either referred to the MMC or cleared by the Secretary of State.

If a takeover or merger is referred to the Monopolies and Mergers Commission within four months of being put into effect and the MMC finds that it will operate or may be expected to operate against the public interest, then 'corrective action' may be required. The powers vested in the Secretary of State include the ability to order divestiture of the company acquired. This draconian sanction explains why, in general, a referral to the MMC is seen as a good reason to suspend or cancel a proposed acquisition.

A further constraint on acquisition agreements is the UK competition law as set out in the Restrictive Trade Practices Act 1976. This is likely to have an impact on private purchase agreements, especially where substantial sums are being paid for goodwill or where a 'people business', that is a business dependent for its success on its staff, is the subject of the acquisition. Restrictive covenants and their application and enforcement form a topic worthy of a separate book. Here I merely flag the danger and also mention that an agreement containing restrictive covenants may be registered with the OFT. If it is not, the restrictions will be void and unenforceable.

The Treaty of Rome also addresses competition. Article 85 prohibits or automatically renders void undertakings which prevent, restrain or distort competition. Article 86 prohibits abuse by one or more undertakings of their dominant market position. Companies and directors of companies who ignore orders from the European Commission to rectify any breaches to Article 85 or 86 can be, and have been, fined.

The European Commission Merger Control Regulations came into force on 21 September 1990 and can apply in some unexpected circumstances. Again, if in doubt the only safe course is to apply to the Commission for an advance consent or clearance. Failure to obtain advance approval can jeopardise the validity of the whole transaction. If formal notification is necessary, then the Commission will usually give a ruling within a few weeks. If the view is that a transaction may be anti-competitive, then the full investigation may take three or four months to complete.

The regulations apply where there is a merger of two previously independent businesses and there is a Community dimension to the transaction. Here again, the ability to exercise decisive influence over the other party is a test of whether or not a merger takes place. The Community dimension test is somewhat clearer than that in the Fair Trading Act 1973, being whether:

- the combined aggregate worldwide turnover of the undertakings concerned exceeds 5,000 million ecus; *and*
- the aggregate community-wide turnover of each of at least two of the undertakings exceeds 250,000 million ecus, unless each of the undertakings concerned achieves more than two-thirds of its aggregate community-wide turnover within one and the same member state.

Where more than two-thirds is within one state or the business is one seen as the preserve of national governments – for example, defence – then the matter may be referred back to the relevant national body, the MMC in the United Kingdom.

A joint venture may come within the scope of EU regulations if deemed to be subject to the joint control of its parents. While the regulations were not intended to control cooperation agreements between undertakings which remain independent, guidelines intended to clarify the matter and case law have created a minefield. If you attempt a joint venture which may be caught by these regulations, ensure that you set out with an adviser experienced in navigating this particular area.

If there is an agreement for a full-scale merger of two businesses, or if joint control of a company is acquired, notification must be made by both parties to the merger or those acquiring joint control. In the case of the acquisition of the controlling interest in one company by another, only the bidder or acquirer need complete the form of notification. In any case, a representative to act on behalf of those making notification to receive correspondence and to accept service of the documents must be appointed. There must be an address for service of documents in Brussels.

The notification must be submitted on the official form within seven days of the signing of the merger agreement or of the announcement of a public bid. The form must be in one of the EU official working languages (English, German or French) and set out in the prescribed format. If supporting documents are in another language, a translation must be provided. If any of the information requested is unavailable – on the target of a hostile bid, for example – then the reasons for its absence should be detailed when submitting the form to seek release from the obligation to provide full information. Without such release from the Commission, the time periods will not start to run.

The information required is complex and its completion can be a costly burden. It is necessary to have as much as possible prepared well in advance to be able to comply with the seven-day timetable from signature of contract or bid announcement. If the form is not fully provided with the information requested the time periods will not start to run and may be suspended at any time. The information required includes:

● the parties,
● their representatives,
● the nature of the transaction,
● financial and economic details,
● analysis of turnover by geographic areas (that is world-wide, EFTA, EU and member state),
● history of ownership and control of other undertakings,
● details of acquisitions made within the last three years,
● detailed information on markets by relevant product and geographic area,
● explanation and justification of the market definitions used,

- information on the main competitors,
- price comparisons for the products, and
- barriers to market entry.

This list is not exhaustive but is set out to emphasise the need for thorough advance preparation.

Where any party to a deal has a significant share of its market in a given country or jurisdiction, it is wise to check out at an early stage whether there is any relevant legislation. Procedural details vary but many countries have legislation to control cartels, anti-trust activity or to prevent monopolies. In the United States the Hart-Scott-Rodino Anti-Trust Improvements Act 1976 gives the Department of Justice's Federal Trade Commission time to obtain information and to consider the proposals by imposing a 30-day waiting period, after the filing of a formal notification, before any acquisition above the stipulated threshold may go ahead. An example of a jurisdiction covering more than one country is that of the EFTA countries where the European Area Agreement, which came into force on 1 January 1994, provided for the control of mergers. This legislation is generally similar to the EU Merger Control Regulations.

Careful timing can save money

A major deal needing a Super Class 1 circular will need:

- a forecast;
- an accountants' letter concerning due diligence over the directors' statements;
- an opinion from the directors, confirmed by the accountants, as to the sufficiency of working capital available to the business in the future in its new form;
- an indebtedness statement at the latest practicable date.

All these take a lot of time and effort to put together. But much of this information is prepared in a listed company at regular intervals, certainly half-yearly and often quarterly, even if only for internal information. So all other things being equal, if the timing of a prospectus can be so arranged to coincide with a normal forecasting period, then much duplication of effort can be avoided. In addition, confidentiality is easier to maintain. No one in the divisions is surprised if head office forces the pace a little more than usual on the half-yearly results. A repeat performance just one month later, especially accompanied by requests for indebtedness, may cause undesirable speculation.

The banking covenants, the debenture deeds, the share classes

We are back to more reading of legal documents here. In each of these classes of document – all concerned with funding the operations of the business – those providing the funds will have built-in clauses to protect themselves from major change and surprise. Now is the time to read the covenants and to assess the impact of the proposed actions thereon. If the proposed acquisition is one where significant access to the other party's documentation is provided at this stage, it is also important to check for change of control triggers within the banking and funding documentation for the target as well. However, in many cases access to that information is not available at this early stage.

Often the proposed changes will trigger a cancellation of the arrangements or a need to seek approval from the other party concerned. Before seeking such approval, the impact of the insider dealing rules and the communication of price-sensitive information must be considered. If the proposals are well argued and have sound business underpinning, then the necessary advice, negotiation and consent for the change should not be a difficult problem. There are, of course, cases where a proposed diversification is into a field which is an anathema to a particular bank; in such a case alternative funding may need to be arranged. 'The credit committee will not like it' means polish up your best sales pitch and most persuasive manner and information. 'The credit committee will not touch that sector' means that you start checking out their competition.

Change of control clauses can also lurk within distribution agreements, software licences and a multitude of other types of agreement. If any contract is of importance to the business, then it should be ascertained in advance that the other contracting party will not exercise its right to terminate as and when the acquisition takes place. Where such a contract is crucial to the business being acquired, approval of the change of control or the novation of the contract as appropriate should be made a condition precedent of the purchase.

Joint ventures and investments

Many joint venture agreements contain change of control provisions and these must be addressed as with other similar contracts. In some jurisdictions there are forms of exchange and investment control which will require clearance if the ultimate holding company of the registered owner of certain investments changes. For instance, investments of a certain size in quoted Australian companies need clearance from the Foreign Investment Review Board in Australia for a change of ultimate owner; if not, sanctions are imposed. Again, the timetable must allow a realistic amount for the application and response. Such consents can be added to the list of preconditions for completion.

Industry-specific legislation

A further area for review is that of any legislation or regulation which specifically relates to the industries in which the company or companies concerned in the proposed actions are concerned. Television companies will need to study the constraints in the Broadcasting Act 1990 and its amending legislation. Companies in retail finance will need to consider the Consumer Credit Act 1974, the Financial Services Act 1986 and the other legislation which impacts on their business. Higher and further education establishments will need to consult their Funding Council. In most cases the secretary will already be alive to the requirements of the relevant legislation or regulatory environment. However, where an acquisition is proposed of a company in an environment subject to such regulation it is time for some more homework.

Regulation can have some unexpected side-effects. How do you persuade the public to buy shares in a company that makes products which cannot be advertised? That was the question which confronted Seita, the French, state-owned tobacco company when planning its privatisation. Under the *Loi Evin* passed in 1993, it was illegal to advertise tobacco products except in trade journals. Seita devised an imaginative advertising campaign which aimed to make a virtue out of the constraints facing tobacco vendors. It then found itself facing an inquiry by the Paris prosecutor's office into whether the law had been broken. The robust response from Seita saw the inquiry as bringing some extra publicity.

Companies Act requirements

Conduct by companies is generally regulated by the Companies Act 1985 ('the Act') as amended by the Companies Act 1989 and subsequent legislation. We considered earlier the transactions for which the Yellow Book requires a meeting to obtain the consent of the shareholders of a listed company to the proposed transaction. Very similar rules apply to companies quoted on the Alternative Investment Market. Any limited company may need shareholder approval where all or part of the consideration for a transaction is to be satisfied by an issue of shares. Unless the consideration can be satisfied within the existing authorised share capital and within the numbers of shares already approved by the shareholders for allotment, then resolutions to create and to authorise the allotment of the relevant shares will be required under sections 121 and 80 of the Act respectively. Where there are pre-emption rights, then sections 89 and 90 of the Act must be complied with or the shareholders must resolve to waive their rights.

If one or more of the directors of a selling company is connected to the buyer, as is usual if the transaction is a management buy-out, then shareholder approval may be necessary under the specific provisions of section 320 of the Act.

Check your Articles

Of course, every director and secretary has a copy of the company's Articles of Association, and each of you knows their provisions. In most cases they can bear a spot of revision. Check the rules governing board meetings and, where telephone meetings are permitted, check that the technology available matches any detailed requirements within the Articles. Do not risk submitting certified minutes of a meeting to a bank, the Stock Exchange or the other side's lawyers and then to be asked for the sight of the Article authorising that form of board meeting – only to find that it does not exist in that form.

Check the rules relating to general meetings. If the action you are proposing is controversial, or if you are the target in a hostile bid, check the ways in which you are permitted to minimise the mischief-making capabilities of shareholders at general meetings. If you are a hostile bidder, check the target's Articles as well as your own. The Articles of a limited company are a matter of public record. Your advisers should have the other party's Memorandum and Articles of Association as a matter of course and, if you want your own copy, a telephone call to Companies House with your account number or credit card number handy will provide what you need.

If you have more than one class of share in issue, check the rules concerning meetings of class actions. The levels of quorum required for many classes of security are extremely high. Give advance warning if you need to build the extra week or ten days into the timetable to allow for the almost inevitable adjournment because inquorate and reconvening later at a meeting at which the quorum requirements maybe less stringent. Also check the requirements of any trust deed for debenture holders or unsecured loan stock holders. Is there any covenant within the deed which would trigger a class meeting and if so, what are the requirements for such a meeting? Not only may the quorum be inconveniently high but the notice may well be a full 28 days.

Many years ago, having struggled to get the financial accounts completed for a company in difficult trading circumstances, we realised in April that we had breached a covenant within the unsecured loan stock deed. With a 28-day notice requirement and a need for delicate negotiations with the trustee, it proved impractical to hold the meeting of unsecured loan stockholders until the last week in May. The meeting had an added piquancy because we had hired the upstairs room of a City institution, where a receiver had hired the larger downstairs hall for a creditors' meeting on the same day. Our loan stock-holders, aware of bad news and disappointing results, were somewhat disconcerted to be greeted at the entrance door with a large notice signposting a 'Creditors' meeting'. A certain amount of reassurance was even more necessary than had been anticipated before they passed the resolution containing the agreement to become debenture holders. We then spent the Friday night of a bank holiday weekend at the printers proof-reading. We succeeded in achieving a Certificate of Posting for the report and accounts dated Saturday, 29 May. To our great relief, the Stock Exchange did not take issue with the fact that Monday was a bank holiday and our accounts were required to be published under the Continuing Obligations imposed by the Yellow Book before the end of May, which was 'within six months of the end of the financial year'.

Are you planning to issue a prospectus and to seek a listing for the new shares? In a flotation or for the issue of a new class of shares the Articles of Association of the company must comply with the criteria set out in Chapter 13 of the Yellow Book. As the requirements are now updated on a regular basis, many existing listed companies will find that their Articles of Association no longer comply in every respect. Under the Listing Rules the company solicitors are required to confirm compliance with Chapter 13 to the Stock Exchange.

Those who are well organised will update their Articles to comply with the current requirements at the annual general meeting before a share issue takes place. The less well organised will have to seek the approval of shareholders for the changes at an extraordinary general meeting to approve the share issue. If the changes are minor ones, it may be possible to obtain the consent of the Stock Exchange to proceed on the basis of a commitment to bring the Articles into line at the first possible opportunity, usually the next annual general meeting.

Advanced section 212

We have already reviewed earlier the need to have your enquiries as to ultimate shareholders under section 212 of the Companies Act 1985 up to date and in good working order. However, the person working on this on a daily basis can provide a much more useful service if properly briefed. This is most critical for the subjects of a bid but is also useful for any company whose shares are likely to be scrutinised in a period of great activity.

When matters become critical it is possible to issue much more stringent section 212 demands and to put very tight time-scales on them. There is a story of one assistant company secretary who demanded and got a reply by telex within twelve hours. When my company's shares soared from £4.50 to nearly £6.00 in the space of a couple of weeks I even served section 212 notices on the market makers. They did not like it but they complied. At the very least this advises you which brokers have been promoting your shares. During the government's sale of its remaining stake in PowerGen and National Power in 1995, it was announced that section 212 notices had been served on SEPON (see Glossary) in an attempt to discover the market makers' positions. This was against a background of increasing regulation and disclosure designed to prevent share price manipulation.

A familiarity with the addresses of both a potential bidder and its advisers can also highlight possible undesirable activity to be investigated. Certain nominee companies are known to secretaries and advisers as frequent repositories for undisclosed principals.

Employment

If a company is purchased, then the obligations of that company as an employer to its employees are acquired within the company. These are only avoided if all employees have voluntarily resigned before the transaction takes place. Even in that case, it would be prudent to obtain some form of indemnity from the vendors for any liabilities which may arise.

If a business is purchased, the position is less clear. The original directive concerning employment when an undertaking is transferred was passed into UK law as the Transfer of Undertakings (Protection of Employment) Regulations SI1981/1794 in 1982 ('TUPE') and debate has raged ever since as to the meaning and the effect of the regulations. These were substantially amended by the Trade Union Reform and Employment Rights Act 1993 ('TURER') and subsequent case law. At the same time, the European Commission has been working on a revised draft of the Directive itself. This attempts to distinguish between the transfer of an undertaking and that of the activity of an undertaking.

Much of the controversy concerns the definition of a relevant transfer – that is, the transfer of a business or part of a business to which the Regulations or TURER apply. Early advice should be sought from an expert in employment law if an acquisition of a business includes the transfer of employees.

Where a relevant transfer has taken place, the Regulations not only have the effect of transferring the contracts of employment to the transferee employer but also (with certain exceptions) the transferor's rights and obligations thereunder are also transferred. This liability extends to acts of the transferor before transfer except for criminal liability. As a result of case law it is now generally accepted that if the transferring employer dismissed employees before a relevant transfer, then (with very limited exceptions) the transferee employer assumes the resultant liabilities and any claims by employees would be against the new employer. It is not even permitted for the employee to contract out of such a transfer, and the courts disregard any such terms in a new contract. The extent to which restrictive covenants can be enforced under a transfer of undertakings is also a vexed question. The problem exists; it can prove expensive to the purchaser of a business. Thus expert advice in the light of the facts of the case is indispensable.

Pension schemes

Many companies provide occupational pension schemes, either final salary schemes where pension benefits are linked to earnings or money purchase schemes where the commitment is to the level of contributions paid into the scheme. In addition, some employers sponsor individual pension plans and unfunded arrangements, especially for senior staff caught by the earnings cap. While TUPE explicitly excluded pension rights, an Employment Appeal Tribunal has required the protection of pension interests at the time of the transfer of the business in *Walden Engineering Co. Ltd.* v. *Warrener* [1993] IRLR 420. There is though no obligation on the new employer to continue to provide pension benefits comparable with those provided by the employer from whom the employment was transferred.

The majority of company schemes are Inland Revenue approved and subject to the regulations policed by the Pensions Schemes Office within the Inland Revenue. Those schemes which have contracted out of SERPS are also regulated by the Occupational Pensions Board which is within the Department of Social Security. The trustees to the schemes of the buyer and the seller will have different responsibilities. Those trustees who are also directors of the employing companies frequently find themselves wearing two hats and resolving conflicts of interest during the conduct of routine pension matters. These conflicts are compounded when a takeover occurs and many trustees will need independent professional advice on their legal responsibilities under the relevant trust deed as well as on actuarial matters.

Given the complexity of the legislation and regulations governing pensions and the uncertainties of funding which depends on projections of future events, expert advice is essential at an early stage of negotiation and before all later steps are taken to complete any acquisition. The obligations of pension schemes are also a moving target as statute, directives and case law alter the positions concerning indexation, discrimination between different groups of employees and other matters. The inherent delays in ensuring that any scheme transfer is properly conducted result in a further complication. This is known as the participation period during which employees of the purchased company continue as members of the seller's pension scheme for a time after the completion of the sale, at which point they become employees of the buyer's group.

Advice on pension matters is beyond the scope of this book other than to warn that the pension position should be investigated by experts as early as possible in the due diligence procedures, and that expert actuarial and legal advice should be sought by all parties at all stages.

CHAPTER 5

Who's who in the City

The Stock Exchange

The London Stock Exchange is frequently referred to by those based in the United Kingdom who deal in stocks and shares just as 'the Exchange'. It is the main market for stocks and shares in the United Kingdom. The corporate activities of flotation and new share issues are among those where the Exchange fulfils its primary market function. Companies, the UK government and other organisations use the stock market to raise capital or to borrow money from investors by issuing securities at a set price to those investors in exchange for cash. Bringing together the buyers and sellers of securities already issued is its secondary market function.

The London Stock Exchange grew from informal markets in stocks and shares within the City of London during the seventeenth and eighteenth centuries. In 1773 the members of one of the most successful groups voted to change its name to the Stock Exchange and, in May 1801, it moved to the site at Stock Exchange Tower which still houses its administrative offices. Over the years the government has sought to regulate the market and to protect investors. In 1877 the government set up a Royal Commission 'to inquire into the origin, objects, present constitution, customs and usages of the London Stock Exchange'. In 1890 an Association of Stock Exchanges in the United Kingdom was formed of more than twenty stock exchanges across the country. By 1973, the increasingly close cooperation of these exchanges led to the amalgamation of all stock exchanges in the United Kingdom and Ireland into the body still known as the London Stock Exchange. After the Second World War a Compensation Fund against the failure of any member firm was introduced and the degree of regulation of member firms and their partners gradually increased.

In the 1970s the Restrictive Trade Practices legislation was extended to cover service industries, and in 1979 exchange controls were abolished. Pressures from increasing global competition and the initiation of court action concerning the Exchange's Rule Book by the Office of Fair Trading led to another major change, commonly known as the 'Big Bang'. This led to the abolition of a scale of minimum commissions and of the Compensation Fund, abolition of the separation of capacity between broker and jobber, and changes in the rules relating to ownership of member firms and voting rights. A computer-based price quotations system known as Stock Exchange Automated Quotations (SEAQ) was also introduced giving real-time share price information. Following European legislation and the Financial Services Act 1986 the Exchange took on certain regulatory powers. Those of interest to companies accessing the primary market are laid down in the Yellow Book.

Yellow Book

The Yellow Book, formally 'The Listing Rules', is published by the Council of the International Stock Exchange of Great Britain and Ireland. For any listed company, the Yellow Book forms one of the bibles by which matters relating to the Stock Exchange must be conducted. Inevitably, the rules change from time to time. At that point everyone concerned is on a learning curve – advisers as well as the directors and company secretary. The company is usually on a learning curve as there have always been changes in custom and practice if not in the actual rules since the last time one did a similar deal. In 1984, convinced that my company had paid for the learning curve of both its lawyers and merchant bankers with the new edition of the Yellow Book, I swore that I would never again do a deal with a new Yellow Book. However, business does not permit the luxury of the adjustment of timing to avoid revisions of the rules. MAI plc bid for Anglia Television very soon after the new Yellow Book came into force on 1 December 1993. The timing was dictated by changes in legislation relating to broadcasting companies and commercial considerations and took no account of the changes to the technical hoops through which one must jump.

This edition of the Yellow Book has been completely rewritten and is in a new format, A4 in size, but remains loose-leaf and in one volume. The Stock Exchange intended that the redrafting should provide a book capable of being read and understood by the company secretary of a listed company who may be an infrequent user rather than just by an experienced practitioner. This has largely been achieved. A regular six-monthly review, consultation and update programme is now in place. All users have an opportunity to comment on proposed changes and it is important to make sure that one's copy is kept up to date. Although there are now 25 chapters compared to 10 sections in the previous edition, it is much easier for the occasional user to find the relevant section and to understand it once found. The Yellow Book is an essential tool in conducting the business of a listed company or indeed any business involving the shares of a listed company.

The Panel and the City Code

The Panel on Takeovers and Mergers, commonly known as the Panel or the

Takeover Panel, is the regulatory body which publishes and administers the City Code on Takeovers and Mergers. The Code is designed to ensure good business practice and fairness to the shareholders of companies the shares of which are held by the public. The maintenance of fair and orderly markets is a crucial element of the Panel's work. The Panel was set up in 1968 as a non-statutory body in response to mounting concern about unfair practices. Its composition and powers have evolved over the years to reflect changing circumstances. The Code applies to all offeree or potential offeree companies resident in the United Kingdom, the Channel Islands or the Isle of Man and also to such companies resident in the Republic of Ireland if they are listed or dealt with on markets controlled by the London Stock Exchange. The Code also applies to certain private companies, as mentioned earlier. It is a requirement of the Stock Exchange that the provisions of the Code should be observed by listed companies in relation to their securities. Companies traded on the Unlisted Securities Market, the Alternative Investment Market or otherwise traded under rule 535.2 of the Stock Exchange will also be covered by the Code.

The Code aims to ensure:

- equality of treatment between shareholders of whatever size;
- adequate and timely information about an offer;
- a fair market in the shares of companies which are involved in takeovers;
- equality of information whereby all bidders must receive the same information about the company;
- that if control of a company, considered to be 30 per cent of the voting rights, is acquired, a mandatory bid must be made to all other shareholders; and
- that target companies do not take action which would frustrate an offer against the wishes of their shareholders.

As it says in its annual report,

> the essential characteristics of the Panel system are flexibility, certainty and speed, enabling parties to know where they stand under the Code in a timely fashion. It is important that these characteristics should be retained in order to avoid over-rigid rules and the risk of takeovers becoming delayed by litigation of a tactical nature, which may frustrate the ability of shareholders to decide the outcome of an offer.

The flexibility of interpretation and speed of reaction essential in the fast-moving world of takeovers is an attribute of the non-statutory nature of the Panel. The Panel encourages early and frequent consultation of both practitioners and companies so that problems can be avoided. It is always prepared to provide guidance and to discuss problems in context and in a realistic way. It monitors takeovers, including all actions taken, documents issued and announcements made, to ensure that they comply with the Code and keeps a close watch on dealings in the relevant securities.

The Code is not part of the law. However, compliance with its provisions will be taken into account by a court assessing the reasonableness of actions taken or not taken. Where breaches occur, disciplinary action may range from private reprimand through public censure to formal reporting to another relevant regulatory authority. The Code, also known as the Blue Book, is subject to revision from time to time. An up-to-date edition is one of the essential items of equipment for any company involved in any way in a takeover which is subject to the Code.

Merchant bankers

Merchant bankers, known in the United States as investment bankers, are essentially banks which have decided to specialise in corporate finance. The prime aim is to help to raise money to fund business. This includes sponsoring capital issues and the sale of securities to the public. The merchant banker advises the company on the best way to achieve its objectives. Because of its wide experience of such transactions the merchant bank will also review the proposed strategy for viability and advise on ways to achieve it in current markets. They are the middle men.

Middle men are expensive but necessary. We all know how difficult it is to negotiate and to avoid becoming emotional when your personal position is at stake. It is much easier to ask for a pay rise or title change for your staff than for yourself. It is easier for an estate agent to negotiate with a prospective buyer for your house than it is for you to do so. It is easier for the non-executive directors to look dispassionately at the merits of a bid proposal than for the entrepreneur who has built up the target company. Directors have a very close relationship with the company they run. An arm's length adviser is a valuable asset.

The banker can sound out people from the Takeover Panel to prospective investors or underwriters on a 'no names' basis. At delicate stages of negotiation they can talk to their opposite number for the other side to sound out 'what if?' without firm commitment.

The corporate finance activity of raising money goes to the heart of the origins of the stock market. In 1553 the East India Company was formed in London as the first joint stock company, in which the public subscribed to own equal (or equity) shares. A modern flotation on the stock market fulfils exactly the same function and the ordinary shares issued are still known as equities. Today there is a vast range of financial instruments, and advice is needed to identify those that are most appropriate for the purpose. The choice will vary depending on when money is needed, for how long, for what purpose, at what risk and at what price.

Any merger or acquisition has to be paid for and unless a company can finance a deal out of its cash reserves, new money has to be found. This new money may be in a variety of forms and frequently in more than one. A modern deal may contain several elements of corporate finance. ASW Holdings PLC proposed in one exercise in 1994/95:

- to acquire 80 per cent of a French company for a mixture of new ordinary shares, cash and debt,
- to invest in a new steel mill,
- to sell an old steel mill,
- to buy back the shares of its 35.2 per cent shareholder for a consideration in kind and in cash, and
- to raise funds through a two-stage rights issue.

The documents issued in connection with this deal were naturally rather thicker than average.

When British Aerospace (BAe) increased its bid for VSEL late in 1994 it proposed a form of rights issue known as a 'flexible trombone'. BAe was able to use this instrument to raise any amount between £178 million and £535 million. The exact amount was to be determined by the final level of the offer and the extent to which VSEL shareholders opted for cash or shares. The existing shareholders were offered the right to subscribe for non-interest bearing unsecured loan stock convertible at the rate of one BAe ordinary share for each fully paid loan stock unit. BAe could increase its offer for VSEL further without having to go back to the underwriters for approval although in that case it would have needed to seek retrospective permission from its own shareholders. Whatever the outcome of the bid for VSEL, BAe received the cash of £170 million for the first part of the rights offer net of costs. As a result of the referral of the bid to the Monopolies and Mergers Commission the second part of the rights issue was cancelled and the loan stock units were converted to ordinary shares.

The following March BAe reinstated the second part of the 1994 flexible trombone rights issue. This was in turn structured as a flexible, two-part issue of convertible loan stock. In addition, BAe promised to issue one warrant for every stock unit subscribed in recognition of the fact that the shareholders were being asked to subscribe for a fully redeemable two-part rights issue under which a second instalment might be called. The terms of the offer contained conditions to cover the various eventualities which might arise once the decision of the President of the Board of Trade was known following the report of the MMC's conclusions.

It is your corporate finance adviser's responsibility to ensure that your lawyer and other professionals are properly briefed. The corporate finance adviser will have been involved in designing the deal under consideration. They must communicate, especially to the lawyers drafting the documents to put the deal into effect, the following:

- what it is that is important for you to obtain from the deal;
- the nuances and background to the negotiations so far;

- any price adjustment issues yet to be resolved;
- any factors which are likely to have a bearing on the conclusion of the transaction.

With a deal to acquire a listed company or a placing, the merchant bank will remain very closely involved throughout. When the acquisition is of a private company without the need for a circular to shareholders the lawyers are much more likely to take the lead advisory role in the latter stages of negotiations and then this briefing is vital.

Stockbrokers

Stockbrokers are the salesforce within the stock market system. Like many other forms of salesforce they are remunerated by a commission on turnover, which will be negotiable rather than fixed since the 'Big Bang'. Much confusion can be avoided and mystique pierced if the basic fact that a stockbroker is a salesperson is remembered. Each company which applies to have its securities listed on the London Stock Exchange must appoint a member firm (or other approved sponsor) to submit its application, to lodge the supporting documents on its behalf and to act as a channel of communication between the company and the Stock Exchange.

In the secondary markets, the stockbroker is well known for acting for buyers and sellers of existing securities of all types. Firms vary in their specialisms and each firm has a specialist team within it concentrating on particular markets or particular classes of stock.

In the primary market function of fundraising it is the stockbrokers who will sell the proposed issue to the underwriters and then assist in selling it to the shareholders and to the marketplace at large.

As with sales houses in other fields stockbrokers employ specialists to analyse the products and provide information to the punters. These analysts are a major source of the information which lubricates the markets. It is important for companies to make sure that the analysts that specialise in their particular field understand the business and provide the markets with a fair representation of the company's business and its prospects. Most listed companies undertake regular briefings of analysts, at a minimum at the half-yearly and annual results times. When some special event is in progress it will be important to build the analysts' briefing into the timetable. It is also, of course, vital to ensure that any such briefing takes the rules on dissemination of price-sensitive information into account.

As soon as a takeover is announced the merchant banker will draw the company's attention to rule 20.1 of the Takeover Code. This rule reflects the general principle of equality of information to shareholders and rigidly restricts the freedom of provision of information and the expression of opinions from the date of announcement of the offer. Meetings with analysts, stockbrokers or others engaged in investment management or advice may take place but strictly under the provisions of Note 3 on rule 20.1. This requires that an appropriate representative of the financial adviser or corporate broker to the offerer or offeree company must be present. To concentrate the mind, that person is then responsible for confirming to the Takeover Panel by the following day that no material new information was forthcoming and no significant new opinions expressed. So the hard-pressed secretaries who struggle with the diaries of the managing director, finance director, company secretary and investor relations person must also ensure that they liaise with the diaries of the relevant adviser and include them in any such meetings. This rule also covers conduct of press, television and radio interviews and stockbrokers' circulars issued during the bid period.

Solicitors

Every corporate activity has legal consequences and any of a size to cause you to read this book will require legal advice from solicitors. Most companies have a regular corporate lawyer and there are many advantages in using the one who is already well known to you and who knows your business. It is nevertheless important to ensure that you know who will be doing the work and that those people will understand what you are trying to achieve commercially. You want someone who can work hand in glove with you, assess the legal implications which matter and who will keep the commercial end result in sight throughout.

Lawyers should in general be involved at a fairly early stage. In some cases they may be the source of the introduction of the parties to each other. If the parties wish to sign 'heads of terms' recording in principle the agreement reached in initial discussions, then the prudent board will have this reviewed by the lawyer for pitfalls before signing. The implications of buying a business or a company are wide-ranging and most firms of solicitors will have experts in each of the relevant fields.

Accountants

Accountants are the experts in number-crunching and in the implications for your accounts and future profitability of the proposed actions. In many cases a company will want to continue to work closely with its existing auditors who already know the management and the business. However, this is not always possible, nor is it always appropriate. There is increasing concern about the extent to which auditors also do accounting and consultancy work for their audit clients for fear that it may compromise their independence. Admittedly the explanation that accounting fees relate to work done in connection with a takeover, merger or rights issue is usually considered a respectable answer from the finance director to a question at the following annual general meeting.

However, where two parties are involved as in a takeover it is a more and more frequent occurrence that both parties have the same auditors and therefore one must go elsewhere for independent advice. A company which is concerned that it may be the target of a bid, particularly a hostile bid, may well instruct and pay a knowledgeable firm of accountants (not their auditors) to produce in strict confidence a mock Offer Document bidding for the company. These accountants would be instructed to tear the company to pieces in a similar way to a hostile bidder, thus helping to identify the many unpalatable comments which such a bidder would make. This is invaluable in preparing a defence. In negotiating the contract with such accountants it will, of course, be necessary to reassure them that no ill-will would attach to their firm thereafter. The more unpleasant their production the more useful it is likely to be.

The first role of the accountants is to act as advisers to the management. The less sophisticated a company, the more vital this function. The board of a top 100 company probably have the in-house expertise to make the sufficiency of working capital estimates. The team setting out on their first management buy-out will need the accountant's assistance to produce a sound corporate plan which will attract financial backers.

The second role is to perform due diligence for the prospective investors. These will range from 'Sid' of the British Gas flotation advertisements to experienced venture capitalists looking at management buy-outs and high technology startups. In some circumstances it is wise to use different teams of accountants to fulfil the two roles to avoid any possible conflict of interest. These may sometimes be different teams from the same firm.

Tax advisers

Benjamin Franklin in the eighteenth century was reputed to have said that 'in this world nothing can be said to be certain, except death and taxes.' Many have achieved takeovers without causing death but probably no one has done so without a tax effect. The tax law is always changing and in a takeover there are a variety of parties with conflicting interests. The deal which is best for the vendor's tax position is rarely the best for the purchaser. And that is before one considers the tax positions of the companies involved.

These conflicts are most clearly seen in a management buy-out where there is a very close relationship between the buy-out team and the vendor. The buy-out team have to juggle their responsibilities to the vendor who is the current employer, the future tax profile of the company and the optimisation of their personal positions.

Before agreeing the structure of a deal, and certainly before entering heads of terms, discuss the proposals with your tax adviser. The tax expert can provide a much better service if allowed to assist at the earliest possible stage. Seeking help to restructure a group only after the acquisition has taken place restricts the advice to a damage limitation exercise. In many cases the tax adviser can further add value by identifying methods of structuring certain aspects of the transaction to the benefit of both buyer and seller. Help in understanding the other party's position and identification of ways to improve it without disadvantage to yourself can greatly help the negotiation process.

Receiving bankers

If you use a service registrar they will have given you the name of the person to contact when you want confidential advice. This is designed to encourage you to use your registrar's services as a receiving banker. Each of the major banks has a department dedicated to looking after the paperwork arising in a bid or rights issue situation. In many cases banks were originally chosen for this task because money was involved. In a flotation, rights issue or other offer the prospective shareholders will be required to make payments – usually by cheque – by a given date. In a straightforward market bid it is the bidder who will be making the payments at a somewhat later date. Whichever case applies coping with the volume of specialist paperwork and payments is an ideal task for a specialist. There is no automatic right for your existing registrars nor for your clearing bank to do the work. There are minor advantages in communication where a service registrar and receiving banker in the same ownership have good lines of internal communications between the relevant departments. I have certainly experienced a situation where the receiving bankers and service registrars were owned by the same holding company and it was clearly proven that the major hiccoughs and delays originated from the target's registrars and not those of the bidder. However, this is not necessarily the case. In some cases where the receiving banking facilities are in the City of London and the registrars at long distance from there communications may suffer.

For a flotation all applications (that is completed forms with cheques) must be lodged at or posted to the receiving bank's designated offices. More than one office or even more than one bank may be provided if large volumes are anticipated, as with some privatisation issues. The receiving bank's specialist new issues office will total the applications and cheques, provide reports to the company and then follow the resulting instructions for the issue of allotment letters to the successful applicants and of letters of regret and returned cheques to the unsuccessful. In the case of a rights issue, the procedures are similar but the offer will have been restricted to existing shareholders. For a bid, the work will involve checking acceptances and pursuing incomplete acceptances with regular reports to the company and its sponsor.

Where a company uses in-house registrars it may prefer to outsource the necessary expertise for handling the specialist paperwork at the time of an allotment or bid. In any case it is perfectly proper and becoming much more common to request bids from two or three receiving bankers once the nature and volume of the work is known and to make a decision based on price and quality of service as with any other supplier.

Registrars

Every company is required by law to keep a record of its shareholders and their entitlements. Indeed, under section 361 of the Companies Act 1985 the definitive proof of ownership of shares lies with the share register kept on behalf of the company and not, as frequently supposed, with the share certificate or other paper or electronic record of title. The person responsible for maintaining the shareholder register is commonly known as a registrar. With a small company this may well be the company secretary or solicitor. It is, of course, the legal responsibility of the company secretary to ensure that the Act is complied with in this respect. The law recognises that for larger companies the use of specialist facilities may be appropriate and section 353 permits a company to advise the Registrar of Companies that its register of shareholders is kept at a place other than its registered office. For some companies this will be an in-house service department specialising in registration. For many others this will be one of the large number of specialist service registrars.

During any transaction which involves the allotment and issue of new shares or the transfer of shares between holders the registrar has an important part to play. In the case of a takeover or merger almost certainly two registrars will be involved, one for each party to the transaction. Although many of the practical details relating to share ownership change with the introduction of CREST, the legal basis for ownership and the need to maintain the register of members remain.

Venture capitalists

Venture capital is generally a subscription for shares of some kind frequently backed with long term loan capital. In the United Kingdom it is a business measured in billions rather than millions. Venture capital houses use their expertise to assess the risks of their investments and to invest in a very wide range of businesses, usually unquoted. Venture capital is commonly used for startups, expansion, management buy-outs (MBOs) or buy-ins (MBIs). Thus they are frequently of significance in a takeover or merger as shareholders in the target business. They may also participate as providers of risk capital to fund growth by acquisition. In addition they have a significant role to play when a private placing is the route chosen. In this case, rather than subscribing for new shares, there is a purchase of existing shares by selected institutions. A private placing can sometimes be an effective alternative to the sale or flotation of a company. The 'white knight' sought by the target of a hostile bid as an alternative future owner may frequently be a venture capitalist.

The investor protection committees (IPCs)

These are representative bodies formed by shareholders. The largest are those of the Association of British Insurers (ABI) and of the National Association of Pension Funds (NAPF). These bodies issue statements about changes in legislation and formulate rules which are generally designed to restrict the freedom of action of directors in taking decisions that might affect the value of a company's securities. In many areas the IPCs expect listed companies to observe stricter standards than those imposed by statute and the Stock Exchange. They are often treated as *de facto* regulators although they have no formal control over the companies.

The extent to which a particular listed company will comply with the rules of the IPCs will depend to a large degree on the nature of its share register, its existing reputation and the support which it needs from the various City bodies and institutions. The IPCs have strong views on the extent to which pre-emption rights may be waived and the level of dilution introduced by employee share option schemes. It is usually considered prudent to discuss any resolutions on which shareholders are to be asked to vote in these areas with the most interested IPC before finalising its terms. These discussions can be held by the company itself or its advisers.

The institutions pay heed to the views of their representative bodies, and of others. I have had a pension fund manager telephone me to ask how the ABI had viewed an innovative share option scheme before completing his proxy form. The ABI rules on share options have frequently been quoted verbatim in scheme rules to increase the chances of approval by the shareholders.

NAPF runs a Voting Issues Service which assesses and reports on resolutions requiring shareholder approval at the general meetings of the major quoted companies. This service identifies all resolutions and highlights those viewed as contentious by NAPF. It encourages its members to devise a policy on voting and to exercise their proxy votes whenever reasonably possible. They state that 'this approach helps members to meet their responsibilities and can assist with improving the value of investments.'

Other bodies are also growing in influence and providing advice on voting to shareholders. Pensions Investment Research Consultants Limited (PIRC) have issued guidelines for shareholder voting which reflect strongly the debate on corporate governance. ProShare (UK) Limited is an independent not-for-profit organisation which seeks to increase both private and employee share ownership. It both educates private shareholders and school children on investment matters and represents the views of private investors to companies and relevant authorities. The Council for Wider Share Ownership is also working to increase the number of private and employee shareholders.

Investors and institutions

'Investors' in many cases is a synonym for shareholders or the members of a company. Each company has a different investor profile. Investor relations is essentially a specialist form of marketing. Thus a company should know who its shareholders are and the nature of their trading patterns. Research on large companies shows that only 20–40 per cent of their capital is traded fairly frequently. Thus the purchaser of a listed company is offering to buy assets that well over half his audience have owned for a long time. This loyalty is built on by the defenders of a hostile bid.

The fund managers of the major institutions which run aggregated investments on behalf of numerous individuals are among the key players in the market. Typical examples are those of pension funds, unit trusts and insurance companies. Owning over 70 per cent of the listed shares in issue, these managers are important to the listed companies. For the managing director of a newly listed company the need to keep investors fully informed about their company's performance and prospects is something of a shock after years of answering either to no one but themselves or else to a head office which provided a pro-forma report for completion.

The press

As the United Kingdom is the country which buys more daily newspapers per head than anywhere else in the world we tend to take the existence of the press for granted. If you take the route of the corporate activity involving a listed company the press will become something which takes an interest in you as well as that in which you take an interest. It is essential that your public relations advisers and in-house spokesmen and women are properly briefed and involved throughout so that the correct messages are promulgated. Journalists are human and generally respond in a cooperative manner when provided with some information but in a hostile manner when they sense that their questions are unwelcome. Like the rest of us they have a natural tendency to laziness and a well-drafted press release which minimises the work and research they need do is much more likely to be correctly quoted than a conversation. Of course, they will want the conversation as well to add the spice of immediacy and the possibility of indiscretion to their reports.

CHAPTER 6

Appointing the advisers

Initial research

Professional advisers are required and it can be a big advantage to use someone you know and trust. Many companies will have good existing relationships with financial and legal advisers and sometimes with merchant bankers. Unless a conflict of interest arises the best service, although not necessarily the cheapest, may be obtained by using the adviser that you already respect and who knows your business. In any case, when considering costs bear in mind the full implications of the choice. The cheapest fee per hour does not necessarily result in the lowest bill overall, especially where a learning curve has to be included. The cheapest bill does not necessarily give the lowest overall cost and largest benefit to the business in the long term when all aspects of the advisers' involvement and the consequences of the advice are taken into account.

Nevertheless it may be necessary to choose a new lawyer, accountant or merchant bank. These are the three key appointments for any type of deal whether on or off market. These advisers must be able to work closely with you and with each other to achieve the best result. The run-up to a major deal is not the best time to keep an adviser on their toes by arbitrarily instituting a beauty parade. Much better in the case of accountants and lawyers to have a regular three- or four-year review by a committee of the board away from the heat of battle. If frequent use is made of one's investment bankers, then a similar programme of review of the relationship is probably advisable. However, there are many reasons why a beauty parade will have to be held in the heat of battle.

Conflicts of interest

As there are relatively few major players in each area conflicts of interest arise quite frequently. At an early stage in negotiations it is necessary to confirm that your major professional advisers are not likely to be asked to act by both sides. Where this proves to be the case each firm of advisers has its own protocols to decide whether or not it will be prepared to act for you or for the other party. If they are your regular advisers with a continuing relationship, they will almost certainly help you if asked to find somebody else to look after your interests on this particular occasion.

Sometimes it has been identified that the level of accounting fees received by the auditors is already unacceptably high and may have been the subject of adverse criticism by shareholders and others. When facing a hostile bid as is suggested elsewhere, it is a good idea to ask another, unfamiliar accountant to review your company as if they were acting for the bidder to flush out any 'nasties' which will have to be addressed. In both these cases it will be necessary to choose an accounting firm.

Beauty parades

Before contacting prospective advisers it is necessary to understand clearly what work you require them to perform. It is wise to know:

- what project is proposed;
- its approximate size, both in monetary terms and volume;
- the type of businesses involved;
- any regulatory environments which may need to be taken into account; and
- the extent to which it is likely to attract public attention.

Once the board or the relevant committee thereof has identified the work you require the adviser to do, it is then appropriate to make the first approaches. Advisers who have worked for firms of a similar size or background to yourself in the past or who have been recommended or spoken well of by friends and acquaintances in similar positions will be among the first choices for the shortlist.

Set down in summary the position including:

- any requirements for confidentiality;
- the timetable within which you propose to conduct the review;
- a request to specify their services;
- their position on confidentially particularly in any organisation where reliance is placed on so-called Chinese walls (see Glossary); and
- the basis on which they would propose to charge.

In setting the timetable, ensure that the diaries of those involved are consulted both within the organisation and in outside advisers where these are part of the selection process. For instance, a management buy-out team may well ask their legal adviser to assist in selecting a investment banker or venture capitalist. In recent years it has become much more accepted that the fees for any type of service are open to negotiation. Professional advisers may not yet like talking about fees but they have now accepted the necessity to do so. There is a fine balance to be struck between genuine value for money and a fee level which, while attractive in absolute terms, results in cost-cutting or second-class service.

No reputable adviser ever intends to provide a second-class service. Nevertheless they are human. If the fee negotiation was acrimonious, the result cut to the bone and the appointment was a one-off, then it is hardly surprising that, faced with a list of telephone messages to be returned urgently, the senior partner or director gives priority to an equally urgent message from a valued, longstanding client who is paying a higher hourly rate than the bargain hunter.

Fees

The warning on value for money does not mean that you have to pay the first price quoted. If the job is large, it may be possible to agree a project fee or a contingency fee basis which can then be assessed against the value to the company of the project in hand. Or hourly fees could be based on a discounted scale depending on the volume incurred. It is important to agree who will carry out critical tasks and not to settle for delegation to too low a level within the firm just to save the pennies.

In the case of the merchant bank that is structuring the deal, the fee will usually be based on a percentage of value. It may be possible to fix this or to cap it at an early stage in the negotiations. Capping the fee with an absolute value, or on the price to pay for an acquisition which is viewed as sensible at an early stage, has much to recommend it. Such a calculation will ensure that the merchant bank is receiving a fee commensurate with the work and risk involved. It should be remembered that in their case fees are generally paid only in successful deals and therefore have to include fat to cover the many months spent on those which do not reach fruition and fee-paying maturity.

With lawyers and accountants the fee will usually more closely reflect the time spent on the work involved. An estimate of the overall cost should be requested and provided. Other terms to discuss include the timing and frequency of billing and the extent to which some discount will be granted if the deal aborts.

Other advisers

In the case of other advisers and suppliers such as receiving bankers, printers, mailing houses and the multitude of other costs which arise the principal advisers and in particular the merchant bank will very often conduct the necessary beauty parade, give the instructions and make a recommendation for the selection. It should be remembered that each of these advisers and suppliers is acting on behalf of and is ultimately paid for by the company and not by your adviser. Therefore, it is reasonable to expect to be briefed on the appointments and, if you consider it necessary, to have some involvement in making the appointment.

CHAPTER 7

The action starts

Board meetings

In a properly governed company the strategy which has resulted in the proposed corporate activity will have been laid down by the board. The board will also have been briefed on proposed targets or other activities as matters progress. Nevertheless, there remains the tension between the full-time executives and the board of directors acting as policy- and strategy-makers on a regular but not a daily basis. In particular when an unexpected opportunity arises to take action or to make an acquisition it is most important that the executives concerned remember their responsibility as directors and involve the whole board. For good governance, good relations and public perception it is important that the board is the forum that agrees to proceed with major activity and that is briefed before matters go outside. It is vital that your non-executive directors have their first intimation of your activities from the company and not from the press or worse still from a journalist's telephone call which may subsequently be reported.

When an unexpected board meeting is called and diaries cannot be juggled to fit, it is essential that the chairman and chief executive, aided as necessary by others, consult every director beforehand and brief them as soon as possible afterwards on what transpired.

The board of the company is thus critical for all sorts of reasons in deciding the overall strategies and in taking certain key decisions about timing and price in the course of a corporate activity. However, there are many minor matters and administrative tasks which have to be dealt with in the course of such a major operation. Many of these will require the signature of contracts or execution of documents under seal which will need board authority without necessarily being in that category which the Cadbury Report described as 'matters reserved for the board'. You will already have checked your Articles following earlier advice and confirmed the mechanics for holding board meetings and the powers of delegation of the board.

Usefulness of the committee

The Article which permits the board to delegate some of its powers to a committee of the board or indeed a committee of the board and others is invaluable at this time. Sample minutes of the appointment of such a committee are included in the appendix. The terms of reference of the committee should be clearly set out and the extent of its powers should be clear from the minutes. These should be made clear to the board at the time the committee is appointed. It is well worth the secretary, probably with the legal advisers' help, drafting the minute beforehand. The chairman can then read the minute and summarise the extent of the board's powers delegated to the committee at the appropriate point in the board meeting.

The powers granted at any one stage may be limited to action towards the next stage. Powers may be delegated to negotiate with the target company for a share price up to £4.50 per share. This leaves no one in any doubt of the implications and provides a lever during negotiations when those negotiating must return to the full board for further authorisation.

Checking the timetable

Your advisers, probably the merchant bank, will produce a draft timetable, a list of parties and a list of documents. If they have not already done so, highlight the key dates in the timetable. Every timetable should already highlight and identify by a code letter the date of the announcement of the proposed transaction and the date for the posting of the documents. Most commonly announcement day is known as A and document posting day as D.

All other dates are cross-referenced by being shown as A and D plus or minus the relevant number of days. This convention facilitates calculating the effects of changes in timetable as matters progress or fail to progress. Sample timetables are included in the appendix.

It is worth taking time to familiarise yourself with the timetable and to note the points at which the company's initials appear in the responsibility column. I recall a finance director once commenting that the company's code name appeared surprisingly rarely considering that it had instigated the project and would be paying all the bills. The company's appearance in the responsibility column is rather like that of a swan on top of the water. The occasional elegant appearance surrounded and guided by advisers hides a great deal of unseen hard work to achieve the necessary effect.

When you are familiar with the contents of the timetable identify the areas where work is needed within the company. Make sure that arrangements have been made to get this carried out. Those providing the information wanted do not necessarily have to know the reason for the request. Consider whether extra help will be needed. If it is decided to call on a chartered secretary in practice or a temporary accountant to spread the workload, remember to ask them to sign a confidentiality agreement and the insider dealing rules. A sample agreement is included in the appendix. As the use of professional consultants increases, such confidentiality agreements are becoming common practice.

Has the timetable been reviewed against public holiday schedules, including those of overseas countries or of a religious nature where applicable, and against the holiday plans of key personnel? In the latter case cancellation is almost certainly required. In the interests of confidentiality and good relations the earlier this can be put in hand the better. The sooner plans can be changed the more discretely this can be done and the less the aggravation and associated costs. It is also important to check whether changing the timetable would bring one into conflict with holidays or other closures.

Those deeply involved in the transaction have to accept that public holidays, personal holidays and weekends become completely irrelevant. However, even the most ardent workaholic usually has one inviolate day in the year. I have been asked on Christmas Eve afternoon to call a board meeting for the day after Boxing Day but nobody suggested that the meeting should take place on Christmas Day. I have been asked to summon an emergency board meeting on the morning of the first day of Passover at a company which would not have considered holding such an event on Yom Kippur. And if the chairman's horse wins the Derby the chance of a sober quorum for a board meeting that evening is slender.

When the target has a share option scheme and the bid is in the Spring, see whether the option offer period can be extended post-5 April. Under current legislation, there can be cash flow advantages to option holders who accept an offer in the later tax year.

Discuss with your accountants the flexibility in the timing of the working capital and indebtedness information. Calculate the various possibilities on the timetable and, whenever possible, choose an indebtedness date which will serve even if matters are delayed by a week or two.

Code names

To improve the chance of secrets remaining secret the bidder and target are usually referred to by code words in all timetables and drafts of documentation. A company being created for the first time for a specific purpose will almost always be known as 'newco'. Other code names may be anagrams, alliterations or random selections. I once worked for 'Cupboard' which succeeded in acquiring 'Broom'. When MAI bid for Anglia its 'AIM' was to acquire 'Arrow'. That had an amusing sequel the following summer during the press coverage of a certain share deal. Press sub-editors used 'Aim' and 'Arrow' as puns related to the name of Lord Archer, causing those of us who had worked with the original code names to do a doubletake.

The names may have unexpected side-effects. One newco was bought from a company formation specialist and happened to be called 'Downpour Limited'. The purchasers intended to change its name to 'The Building Management Company Limited' as soon as the purchase of the business of that company had been completed. It then received a worried approach from the owner of a business selling rainwear who had just decided to incorporate. She was most concerned that the company was about to compete with her and very eager to buy the name!

Personal organisation

Remember that you are privy to inside information and must not share the real reasons for a change in work patterns. On the other hand, in the interests of good relations a warning to your spouse and childminder that work is going to be even more hectic than usual for a few weeks should help to make allies rather than enemies. Make it clear that this is important to your career plans and that your reliability and punctuality for social and family engagements will be non-existent for a limited time. Ensure that your confidential secretary has a copy of all aspects of your diary, including evening, weekend and social functions. Brief her clearly so that she has authority if meetings or other commitments to do with the main transaction are required to override any existing commitment. In doing so she should be directly responsible for making sure suitable apologies are proffered shortly before the event. Now before pandemonium breaks loose is the time to decide which engagement should be kept if at all possible, for example the school concert where your child is playing a solo. Also to identify those commitments which require a brief formal apology 'due to pressure of business', such as a school governors' meeting or a committee meeting, and which events can be ignored, such as the photographic club or Women's Institute meetings which you only get to one month in two in any case. If in October you know that the board is considering something which may come to fruition in January, then do not audition for a part in the village Christmas pantomime.

On a practical level make sure you have the telephone number and account number of the taxi firm used by the company in the diary you carry with you. It is also worth having the telephone number of the taxi firm at your local railway station if you are usually a rail commuter. Ring them before the last train gets in and order the taxi to pick you up from home to make your early meeting the following morning if you expect to get home by black cab. Much better than having to get the black cab to drop you at your car in the railway station car park which is the last thing you feel like doing at 2 am. Indeed I recommend establishing relations with your local taxi firm. If you live in the suburbs they may well be a more economical choice for late-night pick-ups from the city centre than a city-based taxi. There is also the reassurance of being collected by a driver you know reasonably well, rather than having to navigate a stranger out into the suburbs.

Taxis may also be worth considering for those who usually drive but are working long and late. A risk manager of my acquaintance is rarely surprised at the announcement of a major deal involving one of his clients. He has often dealt with several motor claims from directors driving home late from business meetings in the previous couple of weeks. Tiredness and tension don't make good driving companions. An alternative is to become a customer of a convenient hotel. For the long-distance rail commuter this may be the only option. In this case packing an overnight bag should be part of the advance preparations.

Do not forget to eat during this period. Ignore any guilt feelings and stack the home freezer with quick to grill or microwave convenience foods. Make sure your diary is equipped with the telephone numbers of the local takeaways especially of those that deliver both close to home and close to the office. If your merchant banker is addicted to pizzas and you detest them, find an alternative delivery service near their premises.

Back-up childcare arrangements are never far from any parent's mind. A review with your partner and any available grandparents of emergency arrangements is well worthwhile. It is at a time when you are under stress that the live-in nanny is most likely to give notice.

Extraordinary general meetings

The extraordinary general meeting to obtain shareholders' approval to a proposed course of action is important. It does not benefit from the long public relations build-up and advance planning of a regular annual general meeting. If the proposal is sound and well argued, the proxy votes will give some comfort and will almost certainly carry the day. It is nevertheless important that shareholders feel that they have been properly treated and allowed the opportunity to have their say.

When matters are not clear-cut or when there are contesting parties involved, then proper presentation at the extraordinary general meeting is essential.

Delegate the job of organising the venue and the arrangements to someone who can be trusted and who has had experience of the company's style of annual general meeting. Individual shareholders like to stick with the same venue and a reasonable time of day. However, this is frequently not possible when arrangements have to be made at short notice. Nevertheless a similar style of venue and a time of meeting which permits those who regularly attend the annual general meeting to get to the venue with ease will be appreciated. The retired private shareholder can be alienated by a meeting at 9.00 am in central London, especially when the AGM is usually held in the early afternoon. If you want to encourage their attendance then a time which enables them to use a travel discount card and to avoid the rush hour is ideal.

It may be worth checking what other meetings are being held at the same venue that day. This could avoid some embarrassment or confusion, as on the occasion I organised a class meeting of unsecured loan stockholders to consider becoming debenture holders because of the company's poor performance and shared the venue with a creditors' meeting. A clash of time or place with a major competitor can also be a disadvantage. Many of the same shareholders will be involved. The worst attended analysts' meeting I have ever seen was that of a property company presenting its annual results the morning on which Rodamco had bid for Hammersons. Later the lunch for the institutional investors was the best attended although the conversation sadly did not concentrate on the affairs of the hosts.

Making the approach

When a public company is involved, the City Code governs every step to be taken. The offer must be made to the board of the offeree company or its advisers and the identity of the ultimate offeror must be disclosed. The steps required are laid down in the Code which must be followed and appropriate professional advice must be taken at the relevant times.

The approach to a private company should also be to the board. For an independent target, the initial approach is properly to the chairman as the representative of the board. The board has, of course, a duty to the shareholders. In many cases in smaller companies the chairman is also managing director and major shareholder. In the case of the subsidiary of a group, the initial approach would usually be a simultaneous one to both the chairman of the target's board and to the managing director of the group. It is common practice for those two roles to be filled by the same individual. Where the business concerned is sufficiently large that a decision to sell would be one for the group main board, then the approach should be to both the chairman of the target and the chairman of the group.

If the initial approach is rebuffed, it can be difficult to decide whether or not to make a further approach. In the case of a private company, one has to rely on general intelligence about the person approached, his or her relationship with the other shareholders and any other information to hand. In the case of a public company, before making the initial approach the board of the prospective bidder will have considered whether or not it is prepared to pursue the bid in the case of a hostile response. The many factors to be taken into account in reaching such a decision will need to be reviewed with the advisers and in the light of the requirements of the City Code. The final decision may well depend on the character and culture of the group and in particular the personalities of the chairman and chief executive of the bidder. Some companies relish a fight; others see the resulting polarisation of attitudes as detrimental to the long-term integration of the target and the character of the group.

If the approach receives a tentative, or more rarely a positive, welcome then the next stage involves discussions of the proposals by both boards and some exploratory talks. Before proceeding with the exploratory talks and the initial stages of the investigation, it is usual to sign a confidentiality undertaking. The target wants proof of intent and protection from a fishing trip by a competitor. The buyer will want to avoid onerous obligations. Any covenants should be limited in time and scope. Rights to disclose information under compulsion of law must be reserved, as should secondary information such as analyses and reports prepared by the buyer and information obtained or available from other sources.

It is often advantageous to carry out some preliminary information gathering as soon as the confidentiality agreement has been signed but before proceeding to heads of terms. A general impression of the target business, the state of its records, the reliability of its figures and the true nature of its business can be gained during a brief visit by an experienced investigator to a cooperative target. Such a visit will usually be confidential to the directors. Its findings can then inform the buyer's attitude in the negotiations to reach heads of terms. It is much easier to build in requirements about levels of disclosure and retentions at this early stage than when the legal documentation is nearly complete. This is also the point for a brief chat with your tax adviser and your lawyer. The tax planner can achieve far greater success for you, and very often for the seller as well, if involved before the form of the deal takes shape in the heads of terms. Too often the tax accountant is presented with the completed deal, asked to save tax and says, 'If only . . .'.

Heads of terms should be kept simple and are usually better written by the principals who know what they want to achieve than by lawyers who obscure them with caveats. Nevertheless before signing, let your lawyer read them to identify any serious defects. Heads of terms, also known as memoranda of understanding or as letters of intents, generally include:

- identities of the parties;
- businesses or companies to be sold;
- the main points of the deal;
- the price range subject to detailed due diligence;
- arrangements for due diligence;
- any special conditions.

The above aspects are not normally legally binding and the act of setting them down will often flush out any major misunderstandings between the parties. Certain aspects will be designed to be legally binding such as:

- confidentiality,
- exclusivity, and
- payment of abortive out-of-pocket expenses.

In English law an agreement to agree is unenforceable. However, *Pitt* v. *PHH Asset Management Limited* 1993 confirmed that an agreement on the part of the seller to abstain from negotiations or discussions with third parties for a prespecified period is valid and enforceable where it is clearly agreed in writing and the buyer has given good consideration for the seller's promise. It is not, however, possible to force the seller to go through with the transaction. Because of this latter point, the buyer tries to add the penalty that if it is the seller who walks away from a willing buyer, then the seller is forced to compensate the disappointed buyer for the out-of-pocket expenses incurred on the aborted deal.

Due diligence

For a public company target, the investigation process is governed by the City Code and is largely limited to that which can be discovered in the public domain and from third parties and by intelligent observation on visits to the company. For a private target the scope is much wider so that a plan is needed about the extent and depth of any enquiries. A group with a large head office may well have the in-house expertise to carry out its own investigations from the commercial, accounting and legal points of view. Even so, when the proposed acquisition is in a different sector or country it is wise to engage specific expertise. A smaller buyer may have some expertise in its senior staff but make much greater use of outside professionals and consultants. If funds are being borrowed from banks or provided by venture capitalists for a deal, then the financiers will have some say in the extent of the due diligence carried out and the qualifications of the investigators.

Initial commercial considerations will have been tackled at the search stage. Further enquiries and an alert ear for trade gossip are usually best made by the buyer's own staff. All involved should be alive to the possibility of the hidden factor or the matter which is not what it seems. When carrying out due diligence for a client I have come across problems unknown to the incumbent management. The opportunity no doubt arose because of the inattention of an owner-manager planning to sell out in the near future. A review of trends and changes in pattern can be much more revealing than absolute figures. Study the balance sheet constituents with more care than the profit and loss account. The latter may be massaged to tell a good story but this must be reflected somewhere in the balance sheet. The latter is a neglected tool in many businesses and may have much to tell an informed investigator.

Where property forms a major element of the purchase then it is prudent to carry out the sort of due diligence that you would if buying the property as an asset even when the deal is to buy the company which owns it. That applies to leasehold as well as freehold. The owner–manager who decides to time his retirement to avoid the bill for dilapidations on the company's leasehold premises is not unusual.

The other area which repays careful study is that of directors and employees. Senior staff contracts can be expensive to terminate in the case of a change of control, and you may wish to reflect this in the purchase price. Union agreements which are more generous than those of the division into which you propose to merge the business can have long-term costs for the merged business. An underfunded pension scheme may prove to be a substantial hidden liability. The relationships between the senior management and the rest of the staff may be key factors in achieving the satisfactory integration of the business post-acquisition. Advance knowledge of these cultural patterns and of which staff you will wish to remove and which to keep can be very helpful in post-acquisition planning.

CHAPTER 8

The documents

The sale and purchase contract

The sale and purchase of shares in a company can be documented by a simple stock transfer form subject to stamping and registration but no other formalities. Some private sales and most Stock Exchange bargains are of this nature. Where an investor offers to buy the whole of the share capital of a company rather more paperwork may be required. The private sale and purchase of a company is usually the subject of a contract as well as the formal stock transfer in the case of a company.

The purchase of assets may involve little more than an invoice. The sale of a business as a going concern with some of its attendant assets and liabilities will usually require a complex sale agreement. There will also be other matters to document, such as the novation of existing contracts and the transfer of employment for staff.

It is worth noting that in an asset or business purchase the vendor company must have power to sell its undertaking. Given that power, then it is the company that executes any sale agreement. Unless the Articles of the company or a shareholders' agreement provides for shareholder consultation, approval of the sale agreement will generally rest with the directors. On the other hand, in a share purchase, all (or at least 90 per cent by value) shareholders must sign the sale agreement.

This contract will usually cover certain items:

- the price and payment terms;
- preconditions and their timescale;
- completion arrangements;
- warranties and indemnities;
- disclosures;
- restrictive covenants.

The consideration

The consideration may be settled in cash, shares, some other securities or any combination of these. It may be payable immediately or by stages. It may be subject to retention or guarantees in case there are claims against the vendors. It may reflect a reduction for a dividend to be declared by the target shortly before completion which would otherwise increase the effective price. Vendors and purchasers, aided and abetted by their tax and other advisers, devise innumerable variations on this theme.

When a business or private company is sold, the buyer will want to make sure that any liabilities arising from the warranties and indemnities can be paid. Retention can take many forms. The simplest would say, 'We will pay you X per cent of the price on completion and the balance on a pre-agreed future date provided that by that date you, the vendor, have complied with your on-going obligations under the sale and purchase agreement and have not breached any of the warranties.' The vendors may well insist on a payment into an escrow account or a guarantee from a substantial parent company. The matter of interest on such delayed consideration will also need to be agreed.

In all types of takeover, payment by loan notes issued by the buyer are popular. These are tax-advantageous for the sellers in certain circumstances and reduce the cash or outside borrowing requirement on the buyer. It must be remembered that the usual loan note deed allows the terms to be varied with the agreement of both the issuing company and a majority of the holders at a class meeting. Where a sale and purchase agreement contains warranties and obligations the buyer may seek to withhold payment to the extent that it claims breach of warranty and the careful seller will have insisted on a provision in the agreement prohibiting the buyer from asserting set-off rights unless and to the extent that the seller has admitted liability.

Where shares in the buyer form part of the consideration, then the necessary approvals by the buyer's shareholders must be obtained before completion can be achieved. If the shares are listed or otherwise publicly traded, then restrictions may be placed on the sellers in terms of disposing of the shares. If a significant number of shares is involved, the sudden dumping of them on the market could have a marked adverse impact on the share price. In considering the numbers which may be significant account will be taken of the normal pattern of trading in the buyer's shares. The company broker is a useful source of help in agreeing these terms. The shares issued or transferred to the sellers cannot be disposed of for a pre-agreed period. When the number is large this may be released in stages. A further requirement may be imposed to seek to ensure an orderly market that when they wish to dispose of any or all of their shares then they should do so through the brokers to the buyer.

When the buyer wishes to pay in shares and the seller wants immediate cash then a vendor placing may achieve a mutually agreeable outcome. This is a mechanism whereby the new shares in the buyer are allotted to the sellers and at the same time the buyer's brokers place these in the market, underwriting any they cannot place. A prudent seller will require the buyer to meet all commissions and other expenses and to provide an indemnity in relation to any third party claim which might arise given that the brokers are acting as the seller's agent once the shares have been allotted.

It may also be decided that the right to use a vendor placing be at the buyer's option and not an obligation enabling a switch to a cash purchase if the share price were to collapse. A vendor placing will not generally require the disapplication of pre-emption rights under section 95 of the Companies Act 1985 as the issue is for shares and not for cash. However, the investor protection committees now try to ensure that where a placing exceeds a certain proportion of the purchaser's share capital, that placing be subject to a clawback offer. In this event, the buyer's shareholders are given the right to call for the new shares, in which case they are sold to the requesting shareholders instead of being delivered to the placees who originally agreed to take them.

Although share exchanges and loan note payments are frequently preferred by both parties, in some cases alternatives may be offered. In an acquisition to which the City Code applies, a mandatory bid made under rule 9 of the Code must be made in cash or with a cash alternative. The borrowing limits and the facilities available will need to be reviewed to ensure that the maximum cash which could be needed is legally available.

When price is based on an earn-out, that is by reference to future profits, the seller needs to check that the contract protects him against manipulation of the numbers, for example, unreasonable management charges. On the other hand, the buyer must manage the business carefully over the period of the earn-out to ensure a proper balance between short-term and long-term benefit. Succession planning is a difficult yet essential art in these circumstances.

Preconditions for completion

Sales contracts including takeover bids for listed companies are frequently conditional on certain events happening. These may include for example:

- tax clearances,
- bidders' shareholder approvals,
- level of acceptances by the offeree's shareholders,
- admission of the new shares to listing by the Stock Exchange;
- clearance by the OFT concerning competition;
- clearances by any relevant regulatory bodies to a change in ownership of the target company;
- consents from any parties to agreements subject to change of control clauses which have been included in the sale and purchase agreements.

Warranties, indemnities and disclosures

These are common aspects of agreements to purchase privately owned companies or businesses. By the nature of the deal they are not available when a takeover bid is made for a public quoted company. The other occasion on which they are generally unavailable is on a purchase from a receiver, administrator or liquidator. These devices are all designed to modify the basic rule of English law known as caveat emptor.

The negotiation of these safeguards has a twofold benefit. The discussions often prompt a seller's memory or cause those who know little about the business they own to make the necessary enquiries to elicit the facts. After completion, the buyer may have a claim if the target proves to have unsuspected problems. The seller limits his exposure by setting time and quantity limits for claims. Time limits generally cover two or three sets of audited accounts except for tax matters where at least six years is normal. The maximum claim is often the level of the purchase price. There will be a *de minimis* provision to avoid administering very small claims and often a monetary threshold which must be reached before any claim can be made.

Wherever the seller's response to enquiry is 'except for . . .' these exceptions are listed in a separate document, commonly one or more lever-arch files, called a 'disclosure letter' given to the buyer as part of the contract. Areas which may be covered include:

- property titles;
- pension obligations;
- intellectual property;
- mortgages, guarantees and similar obligations;
- employee conditions of service;
- contract conditions, e.g. change of control clauses;
- insurance covers.

Reference was made above to English law. In England, and in many other countries, the warranties provide a way of adjusting retrospectively the purchase price to what it should have been had the buyer and seller had all the facts at the time of sale. A warranty gives an assurance that a particular state of affairs exists and if it is breached, in other words if it is not as stated, the warrantor will be liable to compensate the purchaser for any loss suffered as a result of the breach. The damages are limited to those which are reasonably foreseeable at the time of the contract as likely to flow from the breach. A breach of warranty by one party entitles the other to sue for damages but does not afford grounds for voiding the whole contract. An indemnity is a contractual obligation by which one party agrees to keep another protected from a specific loss. Indemnities are used where it is known that there is a contingent or actual liability or loss. Indemnities are almost always used for tax liabilities and also in cases where, for example, the outcome of litigation pending or in progress or the extent of recovery of a specific bad debt are uncertain.

It should be noted that this is an area where Scottish law differs from both

English law and also from the Convention on Contracts for the International Sale of Goods, which governs a great deal of international trade. Its general principle prohibits the recovery of damages by a seller who retains the property and dates from the 1869 case of *McCormick & Co.* v. *F. E. Rittmeyer & Co.* Since 1893 the Sale of Goods Act has overridden this principle for the sale of goods covered by that Act and its successors. More recently the Financial Services Act 1986 provides some statutory protection for the investors in a public issue of shares. For other sales there is no distinction in Scotland between conditions and warranties. The question in Scotland is whether there has been a material breach of the contract which would give the buyer a remedy by rescinding the contract and suing for damages – only granted where there is a fundamental alteration in the nature of the subjects purchased. In December 1994 the Inner House of the Court of Session, the Scottish equivalent of the Court of Appeal, gave opinions which confirmed a decision of the Sheriff Principal in *Fortune* v. *Fraser* 1993 that a purchaser who claims that there has been a breach of contract by the seller is not entitled to retain the property and at the same time to claim damages based on a reduction in the value of the property. These opinions should be studied in detail by anyone drafting commercial agreements governed by Scottish Law. The case concerned the sale of a sandwich bar including the goodwill, stock and the lease with a warranty that the trading accounts, including turnover and profit, were true and accurate. A decrease in turnover led to the litigation. Any agreement for sale or purchase which is governed by Scottish law or which could be subject to litigation in Scotland should be drawn up with advice from lawyers with strong Scottish experience.

Documents to be sent to the target's shareholders

In a takeover bid for a public company a wide range of documents are needed. These include:

- summary of offer terms;
- offer document;
- listing particulars;
- form of acceptance and transfer;
- reply paid envelope;
- section 429 notices;
- consideration cheques;
- share certificates;
- proposals to option holders;
- reminder letter.

The summary of offer terms and offer document are usually bound into one document. The listing particulars could also be included in this document but would usually be kept separate as they will also have to be sent to the company's own shareholders. The offer document is your sales brochure to the shareholders of the target company.

This document sets out the terms of the offer and the reasons why the target's shareholders should consider acceptance. The formal offer will be contained within a letter from the merchant banker making the offer on behalf of the bidder. In the case of an offer recommended by the target's board, the first item within the document will be a letter on the target company's letterhead summarising the terms of the offer, its background and recommending that their shareholders should accept the offer.

The contents of the offer document and the limits within which persuasion and prospective outcomes may be set out therein are laid down in the City Code. The general obligation under the rules is that:

> shareholders must be given sufficient information and advice to enable them to reach a properly informed decision as to the merits or demerits of an offer. Such information must be available to shareholders early enough to enable them to make a decision in good time.

Drafts of this document will have to be approved by the Stock Exchange before posting to shareholders.

In the cases where the bidder's shareholders have to approve the proposals, a copy of the offer document for information will be sent to them with the notice of extraordinary general meeting. In planning the print-run sufficient copies of the offer document duly labelled 'for information only' on the cover will need to be ordered. In the bidder's public relations and secretarial departments it will be good practice once documents are available for issue following posting to have the offer documents marked 'for information only' readily available. The offer documents intended for the offeree's shareholders without that rubric should be kept locked away and only used when it is appropriate to use an actual offer document to a shareholder or option holder of the target company.

The form of acceptance and transfer and the reply-paid envelope will be enclosed with the documents sent to the offeree's shareholders on the posting day (D day). The receiving bankers will appreciate being involved in the design of these documents to facilitate their subsequent processing.

Listing particulars

Listing particulars may be included within a circular with other matter or published on their own. In any other than the simplest of transactions the separate publication of listing particulars is frequently a practical proposition. Listing particulars are the matters which must be publicly published before the Stock Exchange will admit securities to listing.

Where the consideration being offered includes securities for which listing will be sought, full listing particulars as detailed in the Yellow Book are required. These will be sent both to the bidder's shareholders and to those of the target company. Listing particulars may be necessary either as a result of the original terms of the offer or as a result of a revision of the terms during the course of an offer. Where listing particulars have already been published and the offer is revised, supplementary listing particulars may be required. These are normally required to be published and circulated to shareholders at the time of the despatch of the revised offer document. The Stock Exchange may, in properly justified cases, allow the listing particulars to be published after the despatch of the revised offer documents but before listing is granted. In some circumstances where there is a rights issue, open offer or a takeover, a company may send an abbreviated form known as summary particulars only to the shareholders of the offeree company. However it must still publish listing particulars.

The listing particulars document is in fact the prospectus for the shares for which a quotation is sought. The information contained therein is more extensive than in any other form of company report or document. It is designed to provide the basis for an investment judgement and regulations have been introduced and extended over the centuries to enable investors to make their decisions in the light of the best information available.

Where a circular is required by Chapter 10 and listing particulars are required by Chapter 5 of the Yellow Book, a single document may be issued provided that it contains all the information required by Chapters 5, 10 and 14, and that it has been submitted to the Stock Exchange for formal approval prior to its publication. Where the circular is accompanied by or forms part of listing particulars which themselves contain the information required by the appendix to Chapter 10, such information need not be repeated.

In preparing the working capital statement any information on group prospects and any profit forecast must be on the basis of the enlarged group in the case of an acquisition and on that of the reduced group following a proposed disposal. If the listed company is issuing shares for which listing is sought, then the information regarding major interests in shares and that on directors' interests in shares must be given in relation to the share capital both as existing and the share capital as enlarged by the shares for which listing is sought. Thus commitments to take up rights and major shareholders or directors who hold interests in a target company must be given careful consideration and calculation.

The trickiest case I have ever dealt with in this respect was a rights issue which was underwritten by a trust company in which two directors of the company making the rights issue had significant family interests. Very careful wording was necessary to make it clear that after the rights issue each director could have an interest in one third of the company but that the interests were in fact identical and that both directors together would hold an interest in one third of the company. It was hoped that the matter would be academic and the underwriting not required to any significant extent. However, the Falkland

Islands were invaded the day the final proof of the circular was cleared and the issue closed before the outcome of the fighting in the South Atlantic had been resolved. The markets languished throughout this period and the underwriting directors were called on to make good their promises, which meant that the many restrictions imposed by the Takeover Panel had to be observed thereafter.

Documents to be sent to the bidder's shareholders

In Chapter 4 we reviewed the Class tests for transactions. Chapter 14 of the Listing Rules sets out the general requirements which apply to all circulars sent by a company to holders of its listed securities, i.e. its shareholders. Any circular sent by a company to its shareholders must provide:

- a clear and adequate explanation of its subject matter;
- draw attention to any voting or other action required; and
- contain all information necessary to allow the shareholder to make a properly informed decision.

Where it relates to a transaction in connection with which securities are proposed to be listed it must state:

- that application has been or will be made for the securities to be admitted to the Official List;
- the date dealings are expected to commence;
- how the new securities rank for dividend or interest;
- whether the new securities rank *pari passu* with any existing securities;
- the nature of the documents of title;
- the proposed date of issue;
- the treatment of any fractions;
- details of what will happen to any documents of title where new securities are being issued in substitution for existing securities.

In addition, it is required to contain the standard information advising those who are in any doubt as to what action to take to consult appropriate independent advisers; to state that where all securities have been sold or transferred by the addressee, the circular and any other relevant documents should be passed to the person through whom the sale or transfer was effected and, where an adviser is named in the circular, a statement that such adviser has given and not withdrawn written consent to publication of the circular with the inclusion of the reference to the adviser's name in the form and context in which it is included.

A circular which is defined by Chapter 14 of the Yellow Book as being of a routine nature need not be submitted to the Stock Exchange for approval before publication provided that it complies with the requirements of the Yellow Book and that neither the circular nor the transaction nor matter to which it relates has unusual features. Where possible unusual features arise, the Exchange should be consulted at an early stage. If there is any doubt about whether something is unusual, reference should be made to the Exchange. Such reference can be made initially by the company's advisers on a 'no names' basis. It is wise to do this at a very early stage.

The matters now regarded as being of a routine nature and thus not requiring the Exchange's approval before publication are:

- authority to allot shares,
- disapplication of pre-emption rights,
- increase in authorised share capital,
- reduction of capital,
- capitalisation issue,
- script dividend alternative,
- Class 1 circular,
- purchase of own securities,
- notices of meetings,
- Chapter 13 circular,
- early redemption,
- reminders of conversion rights.

Where, however, the document is specified in paragraph 8.23 of the Yellow Book for the purposes of section 154 of the Financial Services Act 1986, namely formal notices and offer notices, then their contents must be approved by the Stock Exchange before their issue. A prospectus, summary particulars and any other advertisement or document (excluding listing particulars) which is issued by or on behalf of the issuer for the purpose of announcing the admission to listing or which is required by Listing Rules to be issued in order to obtain a listing are specified in paragraph 8.24 also for the purposes of section 154 of the Financial Services Act 1986 and must be authorised for issue (without approval of their contents) by the Stock Exchange before their issue.

Generally, the advisers will handle the Stock Exchange approval procedures. Three copies of a draft circular requiring approval must be submitted to the Listing Department at least fourteen days before the intended publication date. When a circular submitted for approval is amended, the same number of copies must be resubmitted marked in red to show changes made to conform with the Exchange's comments and in blue or black to indicate other changes. Special arrangements can be agreed with the Exchange where drafts are submitted by facsimile transmission or other electronic means. To facilitate confirmation that the Listing Rules have been complied with, all but the final proof of a document will have printed down the margin in tiny type a reference to the relevant chapter and paragraph of the Listing Rules requiring the inclusion of the information concerned. Formal approval is given only after any letters and ancillary documents required by the Listing Rules have been lodged with the Exchange.

As with all documents sent to the holders of securities in a listed company, six copies of any circular in its final form must be lodged with the Company Announcements Office of the Stock Exchange at the same time as it is dispatched to shareholders. This may be done by providing a label to the printers, by the stockbroker, by the lawyers or by the company. It is the company's responsibility to ensure that these six copies are filed with the Stock Exchange at the same time as the documents are posted to the shareholders. To avoid confusion and to ensure that the requirement is complied with, as the secretary of a listed public limited company I have preferred to arrange that delivery myself.

Super Class 1 requirements

A Super Class 1 circular must comply with the general requirements relating to circulars set out in Chapter 14 and must be submitted to the Stock Exchange for approval prior to its publication. It must comply with the Class 2 requirements in full, and in addition the company must obtain the prior approval of its shareholders in general meeting to the transaction proposed. Any agreement effecting the proposed transaction must be conditional on such approval being obtained.

The contents must include those prescribed by Chapter 10 of the Yellow Book. This covers information from the published audited accounts of the latest three years, with an accountant's report only where the latest accounts of the acquired company or business are qualified by the auditors. There must also be provided a statement of the effect of the acquisition or disposal on the earnings and on the assets and liabilities of the group. This will usually take the form of a pro-forma statement of net assets.

An important element of any Super Class 1 circular or listing particulars is the declaration of the directors. You will recall that you have been advised that you must know the whereabouts of directors and that each of them must have had the opportunity to consider the contents of the circular and if relevant the listing particulars. This is because each director is required personally to take responsibility by a declaration in the form:

> The directors of [the company], whose names appear on page [ ], accept responsibility for the information contained in this document. To the best of the knowledge and belief of the directors (who have taken all reasonable care to ensure that such is the case) the information contained in this document is in accordance with the facts and does not omit anything likely to affect the import of such information.

To confirm that each director has taken such responsibility the Stock Exchange expects that one of the copies of the Super Class 1 circular or listing particulars submitted to it will have been signed by each director personally or by his attorney.

On one occasion a non-executive director was on a walking tour of a trail on the South Island of New Zealand. His itinerary travelled between huts with minimal modern conveniences and certainly no facsimile machines. The time zone difference and travelling time between his remote location and the head office at London Bridge made the use of a courier impractical. The accountants were already insiders and the help of their office in the town most accessible to the trail was sought. A 128-page facsimile transmission was sent to that office including the latest available draft of the listing particulars and offer document and a detailed form of power of attorney. Luckily, one of the trainee accountants was a keen motorcyclist. She travelled over 100 miles hampered by landslides due to unseasonal heavy rains to a rendezvous with the non-executive director. He studied the papers overnight and signed and initialled them as necessary. She then took them back to Invercargill where they were sent by facsimile and the originals by courier to London enabling the company to meet its timetable.

Form of proxy

Under the continuing obligations in the Yellow Book, a proxy form must be sent with the notice convening a meeting of the holders of listed securities to each person entitled to vote at the meeting. It must:

- provide for two-way voting on all resolutions intended to be proposed (except procedural resolutions);
- state that the shareholder is entitled to appoint a proxy of his own choice and provide a space for insertion of the name of the proxy;
- state that if it is returned without an indication as to how the proxy shall vote on any particular matter, the proxy will exercise his discretion as to whether, and if so how, he votes.

The company will need to make arrangements with its registrars whether in-house or service to deal with the proxies for the extraordinary general meeting in the case of the Super Class 1 transaction. In many cases a format similar to that used for the annual general meeting may be appropriate. However, as usually only one resolution is in question it may be appropriate to have a simpler document in this case. Whichever route is chosen it is wise to consult the registrars to ensure that they are happy with the format and confident that they can deal with the necessary recording of votes. The appropriate return address should always be checked. Too often the solicitor's trainee drafting the document uses the correspondence address for the registrars and not the business reply postcode or else the business reply licence or code has changed since the last general meeting.

The format also needs to be taken into account when ordering labels or envelopes for the despatch of the documents to the company's shareholders. If it is customary to use a transparent envelope or to shrink-wrap with the label affixed to the form of proxy to facilitate identification, then this needs to be taken into account when instructing the printers or mailing house about the terms of despatch of the documents to shareholders. If envelopes are needed, then these must be ordered and printed. As well as the bulk mailing frank mark and reference I strongly recommend printing the registrar's address on the envelope for return in the case of non-delivery. This cuts work both at the Post Office and in the head office company secretariat. It means that changes in shareholders' addresses and status are received at the office which needs to reflect these changes in the company's records.

If a transaction is likely to generate an unusual level of interest, those organising the general meeting will be concerned about the numbers likely to attend. It is possible to include a separate card or a box to tick on the proxy card to encourage shareholders to indicate whether or not they plan to attend the meeting in person. This enables an estimate to be made of the probable level of interest.

CHAPTER 9

Communications

Meetings with advisers

The preliminary consultations with the advisers will involve a high-level conference with the sponsor, the brokers, solicitors, accountants and the company all represented at director or partner level. Later conferences for an agreed acquisition will involve representatives from the target also. At these conferences the principal features of the deal will be agreed. Board approval to the proposals will then be obtained and negotiations will take place, referring back to the boards as necessary. Once the shape of the deal is clear, even if many details including the actual price per share remain to be agreed, drafting of documents can begin. The junior ranks of the advisers with the finance director and company secretary of the company set to work in earnest. One is impressed by the appetite for work of young merchant bankers and solicitors and by the rapid service provided by the specialist printers. I have left a meeting in mid-evening with considerable work to be done on the 'Chinese' as the small print is known. By 7.00 am the following morning I could collect the package with the next proof from the local station on my way to the factory. These drafting meetings require a great deal of background research, all of which must later be verified.

Proof-reading

It is clear from the volume of documents to be sent to the company's and the target's shareholders and the press releases and board minutes needed that a large amount of time will be spent checking proofs. Therefore, ways have to be found to overcome the tendency to read what one expects to see rather than what is actually there. The legal, accounting and banking advisers will make their own arrangements for checking proofs and content. Staff within the company who are concerned should agree a division of labour to ensure that the company has read every word of the documents and that the relevant people have checked the information they have supplied.

Once the documents have taken shape someone with an overview of the situation should read with great care the letters of offer and recommendation and skim through the whole document for sense. This person should not be concerned with the detail, although identification of arithmetic, spelling and grammatical mistakes is always welcome. This person is reading the document from the point of view of the shareholder recipient and above all should be looking to spot obvious omissions. For example, the listing particulars need to include details of principal trading establishments. The compilers of this list may have taken an arbitrary cut-off based on size, which excludes, for example, any existing television studios when the purpose of the current bid is to acquire a further television company. This can then be amended to reflect relevant information. There are rarely objections to extra disclosure.

At a later stage two members of staff who have been holding the fort for routine business in the accounting and legal/secretarial departments respectively should be asked to read the documents to each other. This should also include the checking of cross-references and all arithmetic. Given the volume of documentation if the company is large, this task can be shared among several staff. However, each pair working together should include someone with a numeracy background and someone with a legal background. This review always produces a surprising crop of obvious errors, which have escaped those who have been working closely with the documents.

Directors' responsibilities

When the documents are in reasonable shape they should be circulated to all members of the board. The accompanying note should remind each director that he or she must sign a responsibility statement confirming that the listing particulars include all information within the knowledge of the director, or which it would be reasonable for the director to obtain by making enquiries, which investors and their advisers would reasonably require and expect to find there to make an informed assessment of the assets and liabilities, financial position, profits and losses, and prospects of the company and of the rights of its securities being issued. This responsibility statement, required by Chapter 16 of the Yellow Book, is in addition to that which will be included in the listing particulars themselves. It covers the same responsibility that directors have under the Financial Services Act 1986 and in addition makes it clear that directors owe a duty of care to the Stock Exchange.

If a director is to be appointed as a result of the transaction and that is stated in the listing particulars, then that prospective director is also required to take responsibility for the contents. This may seem unreasonable for someone who may be new to the company or group, but the Stock Exchange points out that a name appearing in the documents can be seen as an inducement to the public to invest in the securities being promoted. Thus the new director must be satisfied that the contents of the listing particulars are correct and be prepared to take equal responsibility for them with the existing directors of the company issuing them. If not, the proposed appointment cannot be mentioned and should not be publicised or made until after any offer period has closed. For this reason the search for and appointment of new outside directors should always be made well ahead of any planned flotation.

Where are the directors?

We have already considered the importance of communicating with all directors and enabling as many as possible to participate in the board meetings leading up to the decision to proceed with the corporate activity in question and to make a public announcement thereof. The further negotiations and detailed production of the documentation inevitably rests with the executive directors. However, in UK law all directors carry equal responsibility for the actions of the company and for the contents of any prospectus or circular published by the company. It is thus important that all directors remain fully briefed and have an opportunity to study the documents to be sent out in their name.

A good company secretary will be aware of all directors' plans and movements. He or she will liaise closely with their offices to make sure that draft documents are delivered in a secure fashion and that diaries can be arranged to allow attendance at critical board meetings.

Verification notes

To protect the directors of the bidder (and of the target in a recommended offer) notes are prepared recording the steps taken to verify the facts and the basis for the statements of opinion, intention and expectation contained in the announcements and documents which constitute an offer to the public or to a set of shareholders. Listing particulars and offer documents are always subject to this detailed written validation. The skeleton of the verification notes is usually prepared by the solicitors but may be prepared in-house if desired. In any case careful preparatory work and filing of documentation showing the relevant calculations and background to opinions as the drafting progresses can save time, effort and fees when the verification notes are completed.

In addition to protecting the directors, the notes also form the basis for assuring all parties concerned with the transaction that the appropriate steps have been taken to verify the contents of the announcements and documents. The notes should describe the source or basis of verification of each statement in such a way as to demonstrate both that the relevant statement is true or that the statement of opinion is fair and that there are reasonable grounds for all responsible parties to believe that it is true and fair. The notes should be supported by documentary evidence and references to authoritative outside sources wherever possible. Where third party evidence is used, those concerned should satisfy themselves that it is reasonable to rely on that third party for the purpose concerned. For example, a claim to be market leader backed by press cuttings based on the company's own press releases would be inadequate; one based on a trade press article written by a university researcher drawing on a variety of sources would be acceptable.

The skeleton notes will list each statement of fact or opinion, including each term of any offer or issue, with the person(s) responsible for confirming it. The sponsor will be asked to confirm its membership of, say, The Securities and Futures Authority, its correct name and its office address. The stockbrokers will be asked to give evidence of any statement about the value of newly issued shares included in the section about the financial effects of acceptance. The accountants will confirm and provide evidence for the sections on financial information, indebtedness and working capital and any pro-forma statement of net assets. The directors, however, remain ultimately responsible for all the contents of the announcements and documents.

In addition to verifying the statements of fact and opinion themselves, the notes must be designed to ensure that:

● no statement is misleading in the form and context in which it is included;
● no material facts are omitted which make any statement of fact or opinion misleading;
● those implications which the reader might reasonably draw from any such statement are true.

The area which cannot be covered by such notes and yet which must be considered very seriously by all concerned is whether or not all material facts have been disclosed. The alert company secretary will usually recall the exceptions to various general statements made, but remembering the critical fact which everyone has overlooked can be difficult.

The notes, the replies to the points raised and the backup documents remain confidential and are not put on display. They are retained as part of the permanent record and at least one copy will have the original signatures by or on behalf of the persons or firms taking responsibility for the accuracy of the facts and the fairness of the expressions of opinion set out in the notes. They are thus available for future reference if necessary and may be called in evidence should problems subsequently arise. Each of the people concerned, including each director, should be provided with a copy of the final signed edition.

Shareholder communications

In preparing documents for shareholder communications during a takeover or merger it must not be forgotten that two sets of shareholders are involved. Thus two registrars will need to be instructed to provide shareholder labels or envelopes. Any printout of labels for posting has to be sorted by postal zones to allow for the different charges. There is another reason for sorting by country when the documents to be sent to shareholders contain an offer or prospectus. Offers of shares for sale or prospectuses are subject to stringent regulation in many countries.

Of greatest relevance to a takeover by a UK company of another UK company are the target's shareholders resident in the United States, Canada and Australia. Local regulations in these countries forbid using the mail for an offer for shares which does not comply with local requirements. These are different from those of the London Stock Exchange and in general are more onerous. It is therefore necessary to make special arrangements for shareholders in these and any other jurisdictions where the offer as it stands may not be legal locally. Any offer document must contain a statement along the lines of

> The offer referred to in this document is not being made, directly or indirectly, in, and this document and the accompanying documents may be not distributed or sent in or into, the United States, Canada or Australia. The new shares have not been and will not be registered under the United States Securities Act of 1993 as amended and the relevant clearances have not been and will not be obtained from the securities commission of any province of Canada and no prospectus has been lodged with or registered by the Australian Securities Commission, and may not be offered, sold or delivered, directly or indirectly, in the United States, Canada or Australia.

Attention must be drawn both in the offer letter under instructions for acceptance and in the detailed conditions to the position of overseas shareholders.

A problem then arises for any company with subsidiaries in those jurisdictions which makes a practice of communicating with its employees on a group-wide basis. Employee shareholders and option holders in the target company have to be subject to the veto on communication. It will be necessary to advise them of the offer and to devise a suitable cash alternative to any shares as consideration.

There are also cases where a company issuing a press announcement or documents to shareholders will be obliged by the terms of debentures, loan notes or other arrangements to provide copies of all press releases and all documents sent to shareholders to parties to the arrangement, for example, loan note holders, debenture holders. Many companies with significant business overseas have local matching borrowings as part of normal prudent management. To fulfil the conflicting requirements of the legal systems the press announcements and documents can be circulated to those to whom the company is obliged to send them. However, they should have clearly attached thereto some form of warning along the lines of:

> We are sending you this press announcement, which we are required to do by reason of our arrangements with you. However we would draw your attention to the fact that the press announcement is not supposed to be circulated in or into the United States and the offers themselves will not be made directly in or into the United States by

reason of US securities law. Accordingly, this is being sent to you as a private matter for your personal attention and is not for circulation or distribution more widely than strictly in accordance with the requirements of the arrangements between us.

Clearly, this can be adapted as required to suit each particular case and country.

Those dealing with shareholder queries must have their attention drawn to the requirements for overseas shareholders. Advice should be sought not only from UK lawyers but from experts in the law of the jurisdiction concerned on the current state of the law in the relation to the particular terms of the offer in question. Generally, where a shareholder accepts an offer for cash consideration or a cash alternative with no shares and provides a UK address, there should not be a problem. Where a fund manager has discretion, provides confirmation of the position in acceptable legal form and can provide a non-North American, non-Australian address for registration, then the company may choose to waive the terms of the offer document and issue shares or loan notes as requested to the investor's nominee.

At times of industrial unrest or terrorist outrages contingency plans must be in place to ensure that offer documents and circulars can be delivered to shareholders, and meeting venues be rearranged. The prudent company will already have included a term in its Articles of Association to cover the eventuality of giving notice to shareholders in the event of failure of the normal postal services. Every effort must be made to deliver the documents and appropriate consultation with both the Stock Exchange and the legal advisers is recommended.

Offer documents to be delivered to the target's shareholders pose a greater problem. With the company's own shareholders it should be sufficient to make appropriate efforts to ensure that they are informed of the business and of the time and place of any shareholders' meeting. With the target's shareholders it is necessary to sell them the idea and to provide them with forms of acceptance and mechanisms to deliver those forms and where relevant cheques to the receiving bankers. In this situation there are clear attractions in using a receiving banker which is part of a nationwide branch network. By arrangement the branch network and internal emergency arrangements for postal deliveries can be utilised although great care will be needed to handle the cut-off times.

Board meetings

The most important board meeting is that which approves the documents and their dispatch. Before this meeting is held the documents will have been approved as necessary by the Stock Exchange, subject to complete and further verification by all parties, and all advisers will be asked to provide their letters giving consent to the appearance of their names and statements in the documents and confirming that these have not been withdrawn. Each director will have completed and signed a statement of their interests in the company and in the offeree. Each person giving an irrevocable undertaking to accept the offer will have prepared such an undertaking for execution.

The bidder will then hold a board meeting to approve:

- the offer document,
- the listing particulars,
- the form of acceptance,
- the circular,
- the arrangements for the extraordinary general meeting,
- the notice of and proxy card for the extraordinary general meeting,
- the working capital forecast,
- the indebtedness statement,
- the estimate of expenses,
- the despatch of documents,
- the application for listing.

In the case of an agreed offer the offeree board meeting will approve:

- the offer document,
- the listing particulars,
- the forms of irrevocable undertaking.

As soon as both board meetings have been completed the London Stock Exchange is asked to stamp the circular to confirm its approval. All documents will then be held in escrow until posting takes place. In the meantime the opinion and consent letters from the advisers will be signed. The documents will be bulk-printed, sorted and packed for mailing.

Staff communications

For a company conducting a rights issue, scrip issue or taking the initiative in a modest deal, the usual channels and levels of communications with staff are probably sufficient. In the case of a rights or scrip issue or any change in the share capital, those who normally handle queries on employee share option schemes will have been involved in calculating the impact on holders and should be briefed to handle questions. Not every circular need by law be sent to option holders but it is good practice to do so as a matter of course. I have already mentioned the safeguards needed where option holders are based in jurisdictions with onerous securities legislation. Once a transaction has been completed with a resultant change in share capital there will be a need to advise option holders in writing of the impact on their options, in accordance with the rules of the scheme.

In a major bid for a business in the same field as the bidder, with the savings from synergy trumpeted in the press commentaries, extra communications with the bidder's staff will be needed. Careful wording is necessary to avoid giving assurances about protecting jobs which may not be possible to keep. Nevertheless, being kept informed of what is going on and knowing that the board and management have the staff's interests in mind is good for morale.

For the target of a bid, and above all that of a hostile bid, communications are vital to maintain morale. Keep divisional executives and those running the outlying operations posted as soon as possible on developments because they will be besieged by questions from their subordinates and workforce. Nothing causes disenchantment more rapidly than middle managers who sympathise with their staff because they all feel left in the dark. Apart from technical questions about share options, two main questions will be raised:

- What will happen to our department/factory/division?
- What are our redundancy terms?

In responding to the second query the company secretary or personnel director must be aware that it is neither possible nor wise to anticipate the attitudes and policies of a new owner.

Coping with the unexpected

In a hostile bid both parties know that neither is in full control of the situation and each will have contingency plans in place. In any major transaction there is the opportunity for things to go wrong. Many minor problems and disasters can be avoided by careful preparation, imaginative forethought and avoiding actions. Late alterations may be needed to documentation if a major change occurs in the business environment. One board meeting to approve the final documents for posting was interrupted by the news of the Argentine invasion of the Falklands. Fortunately, a quick telephone call to my office confirmed that our trade with South America was not of major significance and a statement to that effect was inserted forthwith. The rights issue concerned was mainly left with the underwriters as the stock market languished throughout the war with our shares trading for less than the rights issue price. As the offer closed while fighting continued on Mount Tumbledown outside Port Stanley the underwriters earned their fees on that occasion, taking the greater part of the stock. Several days' delay in posting arose when the bidder for my employer learned that their chief contact at the merchant bank had been arrested in connection with the Blue Arrow affair. His colleague who took over understandably wanted to double-check everything before the deal went ahead.

Stock market changes sometimes require a flotation to be pulled at short notice. The company about to float in volatile market conditions would be wise to review a 'what if' alternative course of action. Companies seeking development capital or looking to quotation as an exit route for its investors can cope with the delay though the disappointment can damage staff morale unless well handled. New Look, the retailer, set up a profits-related bonus scheme to replace the planned share option scheme in this situation. So yet again planning, flexibility and a bit of slack in the timetable can be invaluable.

CHAPTER 10

Posting and afterwards

Posting

On posting day the lawyers will release the documents from escrow. The mailing house will despatch the offer documentation, listing particulars, forms of acceptance and reply paid envelopes to the offeree's shareholders. They will also despatch the Super Class 1 circular including the notice of the extraordinary general meeting, listing particulars, proxy card and an offer document marked for information only to the company's shareholders. They will obtain certificates of posting for both despatches. Supplies of surplus documents will be delivered to the merchant bankers' offices, to the company and to anybody else at whose premises stocks are to be kept.

The person previously agreed to be responsible will file copies of the prospectus with the Registrar of Companies and deliver six copies of all documents despatched to shareholders to the Company Announcements Office at the London Stock Exchange. The merchant bank will lodge copies of all the documents and the Panel fee with the Takeover Panel. The brokers will lodge the application for listing including the cheque for the listing fee and a copy of the listing particulars which incorporate the working capital letter and the indebtedness statement duly signed by all the directors taking responsibility with the London Stock Exchange. A Stock Exchange announcement and a press release will report the posting of the documents. If appropriate, a submission to the Office of Fair Trading will be made by the company in conjunction with its lawyers.

Underwriting

Almost all public offers of securities which will be listed are underwritten. The normal process for underwriting and sub-underwriting is that the sponsors to an issue agree to subscribe for new shares or to acquire existing shares subject to the terms of the offer for sale agreement. Thus provided that the terms of the agreement are met and no catastrophic events occur, a company is assured of raising the cash required whatever the level of public interest. The sponsor then seeks to remove some of the risk and to ensure that there will be a spread of institutional investors by arranging sub-underwriters.

These sub-underwriters agree, in return for a commission, to buy any securities that are not taken up under the general offer. If an issue is oversubscribed the sub-underwriters may not be called on to acquire any securities through their commitment. If the issue is a failure they will, however, be obliged to acquire all unallocated securities at the offer price (or at any minimum tender price).

Underwriting historically has been on a fixed percentage basis of 2 per cent flat rate: $\frac{1}{2}$ per cent for the leading underwriter (that is, the sponsor or merchant bank), $\frac{1}{4}$ per cent for the advising broker and $1\frac{1}{4}$ per cent for the sub-underwriters. Companies are reluctant to shop around for fear that their fundraising plans will be leaked. Cost control is usually limited to minimising the length of time that a cash offer or cash alternative remains available. Research by the London Business School has indicated that the commissions charged for sub-underwriting UK rights issues are excessive. The Office of Fair Trading considered a referral to the Monopolies and Mergers Commission but found that there was no evidence of collusion in the fixing of fees. However, the level of these fees is likely to be the subject of continuing debate.

In general the sponsor and underwriter is the merchant bank or member firm stockbroker although recent changes in Stock Exchange rules have greatly expanded the categories of body that can fulfil this role. Once the issue is public knowledge the brokers (whom you will recall are the salesforce of the piece) sell the proposed securities to prospective sub-underwriters. If the sub-underwriters are slow to come forward, agonies ensue. On the other hand, if the broker is inundated with enquiries the board will be tempted to say, 'If only we had offered one point less return on a fixed interest security or charged one penny more on the new issue.' By then, however, the die is cast and any lessons learnt can only be chalked up to experience. In valuing the security and setting the price the advisers will have had to bear in mind the possible volatility of the markets and the view that prospective underwriters and sub-underwriters are expected to take of the securities coming to the market.

Queries

Companies, their registrars and the receiving bankers need to have arrangements in place to deal with queries. In large transactions those staffing the helpline should be properly briefed and if necessary provided with scripts to cover common queries. In a smaller organisation where those who will answer the queries are already familiar with the documentation this may not be necessary.

In my experience the majority of queries can be answered simply by reading the relevant section of the offer document and the instructions on completing the form of acceptance to the enquirer. It is important that those answering questions are aware of their obligations under the Financial Services Act 1986. No one who is not authorised to do so must give any investment advice and this includes any indication as to whether or not an offer should be accepted. The shareholder pondering which way to vote is perhaps easier to deal with as one can point to the recommendation by the directors.

Many of the other questions can be dealt with by anyone with a basic knowledge of registration procedures. These include cases where share certificates have been lost, shareholders' names changed, probate or letters of administration are awaited and shareholders are on prolonged overseas trips. Shareholders resident overseas may be subject to special rules. As set out in Chapter 9, specialist advice will be needed if the details set out concerning overseas shareholders in the offer document are insufficient for the investment adviser concerned. This is likely to be the case where an offer includes an attractive security or loan note with a cash alternative. A reminder to any enquirer to consult their professional adviser if in any doubt never comes amiss.

The worst tempered shareholder it was ever my fate to deal with was one who had not consulted his professional adviser. He had studied the form of acceptance with a range of options and been nagged by his wife to check with his broker. Irritated, he had assured her that he knew exactly what was on offer and had in his irritation ticked the box for the option which he did not want rather than that which he did want. When the certificates and cash consideration cheques were duly despatched he was furious to discover his mistake. He then vented his wrath for his own admitted carelessness on the bidder's company secretary. By that stage figures had already been finalised and it had earlier been agreed that it would be inequitable and inappropriate to allow shareholders who wished to change their minds to swap between a share alternative and a cash or loan note alternative.

There will also be more formal queries. Various information services who have seen the announcements will want their own questionnaires completed. These cover a wide range of data, including the advisers used and the extent to which turnover in France is affected. The Central Statistical Office asks for full details within two days of the preliminary announcement. It continues to issue regular reminders even when advised that the questions cannot be answered sensibly until sections 428–430 procedures are completed.

Issue of documents to outsiders

The offer document, listing particulars and circular to shareholders are documents of public record. As mentioned before, casual enquirers should be provided with the edition of the offer document which is clearly labelled 'For information only'. There is no reason why these documents should not readily be supplied to enquirers at the company's offices. Those enquiring for forms of acceptance and reply paid envelopes are far fewer, and the reasons for their requirement should be ascertained before their request is fulfilled.

Inspection of documents

The circulars despatched to shareholders and others are weighty documents. Having read the proofs, you may feel that they already contain more than enough information. But a careful look will show that they do not contain everything that a shareholder or interested member of the public may wish to know. Tucked in general information will be a section listing material contracts giving just a general outline of each. Other areas will refer to relevant documents which will be available for inspection during the period between the issue of the documents and the extraordinary general meeting. This period is likely to be extended to the duration of any offer to which the particulars relate. The arrangements for inspection will have been dealt with during the preparation of the documents.

The location of the documents available for inspection must be stated in the listing particulars. The following documents must be available for inspection for a period of not less than 14 days at a named place in or near the City of London, at the registered office of the company and at the offices of its paying agents in the United Kingdom (if any):

1. the Memorandum and Articles of the company;
2. any trust deed of the issuer and of any of its subsidiary undertakings;
3. each document mentioned in 6.C.20 of the Listing Rules (material contracts) and in 6.F.12 (directors' service contracts) or, in the case a contract has not been reduced to writing, a memorandum setting out its terms;
4. in the case of an issue of shares in connection with a merger, the division of a company, the transfer of all or part of an undertaking's assets and liabilities, a takeover offer or as consideration for the transfer of assets other than cash, the documents describing the terms and conditions of such operations, together, where appropriate, with any opening balance sheet, whether or not pro-forma, if the issuer has not prepared its own or consolidated annual accounts;
5. all reports, letters and other documents, balance sheets, valuations and statements by any expert any part of which is included or referred to in the listing particulars;
6. written statements signed by the auditors or accountants setting out the adjustments made by them in arriving at the figures shown in any accountants' report included and giving reasons therefor;
7. the audited accounts of the issuer or, in the case of a group, the consolidated audited accounts of the issuer and its subsidiary undertakings for each of the two financial years preceding the publication of the listing particulars including for a UK company all the notes, reports and other information required by the Companies Acts 1985 and 1989.

Where any document is not in the English language, translations into English must also be available for inspection. In the case of material contracts, a translation of a summary of such documents may be made available if the Stock Exchange has given its prior agreement.

Usually the named place in the City of London will be the address of the solicitors or merchant bank – sometimes both. The professionals will have systems for dealing with enquiries because at any given time they will have several clients with documents on display. Some offices of large companies will have similar arrangements in place. Most companies do not have frequent calls for document inspection. Once a year the directors' service contracts and the registers of their interests must be available for the period between the despatch of the notice of annual general meeting and the date of the meeting. In practice those interested are far more likely to inspect these during the half-hour immediately before the meeting at the venue than to make the journey to the registered office. So the only routine in place will be for the caller to be put through to company secretarial department. A member of staff will then retrieve the file from the cabinet and book a meeting room. If the caller arrives without notice, they may well have to conduct the inspection sitting in reception. In my experience inspections during normal times are either by journalists or litigants.

When a corporate activity requiring a circular is in hand the journalists will certainly be interested. Competitors, clients and suppliers may also take the opportunity to learn more about your business. Most of the latter are likely to visit the advisers' offices where they are less likely to be recognised and their interest will not be noted. Journalists may favour the registered office to get some additional background flavour and in the hope of an unguarded remark. So careful preparation and briefing of security, reception and the staff who will produce the documents for inspection are wise precautions.

The list of documents to be displayed will have been agreed during the preparation of the documents to post. As the company you will have provided many of the originals and in many cases identified their existence. In the case of flotations and rights issues, the company may well hold all the documents concerned and provide the copies to each inspection site. One of the Stock Exchange's proposals to simplify the Listing Rules is to require the documents to be available for inspection only at a named place in or near the City of London or at such other place as the Exchange may determine. Yet again, check the most up-to-date edition of the Yellow Book.

For a takeover or merger this cannot be the case as many of the documents will relate to the other party to the deal. These may appear with apparent reluctance. Where a competitive bid is likely, the restricted disclosure may reflect the aim of putting as little as possible into the hands of any bidder before matters are finalised. This is in spite of the notes to rule 20 of the City Code which say, 'The less welcome offeror or potential offeror should specify the questions to which it requires answers. It is not entitled, by asking in general terms, to receive all the information supplied to its competitor.' Or there may be good commercial reasons to keep certain matters from view as long as possible. In this case one's colleagues may well be among the interested parties who wish to study some of the material contracts on view!

Having agreed the list and got the documents or confirmed copies thereof together in one place all copies for display should be made at the same time. The copies should then be packed in clearly labelled boxes and despatched to a named responsible person at each inspection site. If possible this should be the day before inspection is due. This is not always possible. In one high-profile merger I chewed my fingernails worrying about the possible arrival of journalists before the box arrived from the solicitors the day after the documents had been despatched to both sets of shareholders. We got away with it and the first enquiry to our offices was more than a week later.

Watching the proxies

Every company will have regular arrangements in place with the registrar to monitor the level of proxies for and against resolutions. Each company must hold a general meeting every year – the annual general meeting. You will need to confirm these arrangements with the registrar for the extraordinary general meeting. When doing so, review the details and consider whether the frequency and degree of reporting should be increased for the extraordinary general meeting. Reports could start earlier – although the majority of institutional shareholders who vote do so at a late stage, especially in a bid situation. But the managing director is probably keen to know how shareholders are reacting to the proposals as soon as possible. The early proxies will provide a first indicator of the views of the private shareholders on your proposals.

You may want the reports in greater detail to show which of the major shareholders have already voted. In recent years the institutional shareholders have begun to change their voting habits and a higher percentage now exercise their rights in this respect. The Institutional Shareholders Committee has encouraged investors 'to make positive use of their voting rights' and 'to register their votes wherever possible on a regular basis'. The National Association of Pension Funds first asked its members about voting intentions in 1990. Of nearly 540 funds who replied, only 20 per cent claimed to vote at all times, 23 per cent claimed not to vote and 33 per cent claimed to vote only on contentious issues. In the 1994 survey of a sample of 654, 28 per cent claimed to vote at all times, 21 per cent to have a policy of not voting and 32 per cent claimed to vote on contentious issues only. There is anecdotal evidence that those who vote regularly are the larger pension funds and so the increase in the proportion of shares voted is greater than these figures indicate. Also, a change in attitude if not in actual practice has reduced the number of institutional shareholders who respond to proxy chasing by smugly replying, 'We do not consider it right to vote when we hold shares for our pensioners/ investors.'

Research by Dr Chris Mallin of the Warwick Business School funded by the Research Board of the Institute of Chartered Accountants in England and Wales was designed to measure actual votes cast. The results indicate that the practice of voting has not yet caught up with declared intentions. The mean level of voting by institutional shareholders of the Top 250 companies in the United Kingdom at annual general meetings from November 1993 to September 1994 was about 35 per cent. More detailed analysis provides some evidence that the presence of certain institutional investors, particularly from the insurance sector, may be connected with increased voting levels in the companies in which they have disclosable interests. Levels of votes cast remain low. US shareholders have been exhorted by the US Department of Labor to vote their stock in both US and overseas companies. In her report Dr Mallin quotes one UK company where the US institutional shareholders have voted more proxies than the UK institutional shareholders, not because the US investors had more shares but because they actually voted. When the chairman of Thorn EMI said at their annual general meeting in July 1994 that 42.8 per cent of the issued shares were voted the 'high' level of votes cast was considered worthy of report. At these levels of voting, vigorous proxy chasing remains an important activity in the company secretarial department.

For a controversial resolution at an extraordinary general meeting both monitoring and chasing of proxies will be needed. This should be done in close liaison with the person or department handling the investor relations, especially if the level of proxies against the resolution is significant. I suggest that the secretarial assistant who normally deals with the section 212 enquiries is considered for this work. She or he will have shareholders' details and structure at her or his fingertips and will also have an existing working relationship in this area with the investor relations people. This is an excellent opportunity to involve someone who has probably been holding the fort on a day-to-day basis in the general excitement and to provide some career development as well.

Typically, the proxies are overwhelmingly in favour of the resolution or give discretion to the chairman. There is always the one profit-sharing scheme member or other renegade who votes against the recommendation of the directors on all occasions. Where this person is an ordinary shareholder one wonders why they do not sell their shares instead. When asked, one lady stated that her husband had told her to sell her shares when they reached 25 shillings each (they had then stood at 24s 9d). They never reached 25 shillings and so she never sold. Long after her husband's death she held the decline in value against the directors but would not sell 'as they were not at the price that Lowry had said'. They were Austin Motor Company shares and at her death she was a minority shareholder in a state-owned British Leyland.

It is unwise to rely too heavily on the proxy count. A chairman may be tempted to suggest when a poll is demanded that the result will be a foregone conclusion. It has even been suggested that a poll be demanded if a significant minority present at the meeting is against the resolution to underscore the result by utilising the favourable proxies. Those present may be swayed by the arguments heard and can change their minds. A vote cast in person at a meeting overrides any vote cast by proxy in respect of the same share, *Cousins* v. *International Brick Co. Limited* [1931] 2 Ch. 90. Proxies can be changed by written instructions up to the deadline set out in the company's Articles, usually 48 hours before the meeting is due to start. On a resolution relating to the re-election of a director over the age of 70 at an annual general meeting I have known a shareholder first complete the proxy against the proposal, second following discussions to retract that proxy and submit one in favour, and finally to retract that and formally state that an abstention was in order as it was against their investment committee's policy to vote in favour of any director over the age of 70! If a member has appointed a proxy other than the chairman who then casts those votes contrary to the instructions on the proxy form the legal position is not clear. Should the company query the discrepancy? Written evidence of a change of instructions may provide some comfort but what if the proxy asserts that the new instructions were given orally? The issue was raised but left open in *Oliver* v. *Dalgleish* [1963] 1 W.L.R. 1274. Where the person nominated as proxy does not attend the meeting or decides not to vote, then the relevant shares will not be voted.

Watching the acceptance levels

This is usually of much more interest to the bidder than the votes of their own shareholders. It is unusual for shareholders to vote in large numbers against a board recommendation. The response of the target's shareholders to your offer for their shares is much less certain. A good offer based on sound commercial logic will provide a favourable response in a fairly short time. Under the City Code the offer must initially be open for at least 21 days following the date on which the offer document is posted. This is commonly called the first closing date.

More frequently responses are very slow. The private shareholders consult their advisers, often by post. The institutions wait to see what happens and whether any other predator shows an interest. In a hostile bid, everyone waits to read the management's defence, which should be sent to its shareholders within 14 days, and rumours flourish about possible white knights – friendly bidders on whose mercy the board of the target of a hostile bid throws itself. In a competitive bid the next offer from the other side is awaited and something akin to an auction develops. The bidders may get promises of support from major shareholders at the current level but these are always subject to caveats and frequently part of a bargaining or negotiating position.

The statement of acceptances will be prepared by the receiving bankers on a daily basis. Ask the merchant bank to instruct the receiving bank to send you a facsimile copy directly. This details how many acceptance forms have been received and the number and percentage of shares to which they relate. It will also show how many acceptances were valid but without or with insufficient cover, such as share certificate to follow. There may be a few technically out of order, for example with US addresses or in respect of holdings which cannot be identified on the register of members.

The report will also show the numbers of acceptances for each alternative form of offer. This will be watched with great interest by those who have to arrange payment. The corporate treasurer will want a copy to monitor the levels of cash alternatives and how many of those want loan notes rather than cash. The bank loan arrangements may well have clauses that enable the bidder to reduce the cost by allowing parts of the borrowings set up to be stood down as soon as it is clear that they are unnecessary.

In an agreed offer the offeree board's advice to its shareholders is included in the offer document. In the case of a hostile bid, the offeree board should advise its shareholders of its views as soon as practicable after publication of the offer document, and in any case within 14 days of the posting date. December and April/May with their bank holidays offer some interesting possibilities to the bidder. Kingfisher bid for Dixons shortly before Christmas 1989 and Dixons successfully obtained an extension from Boxing Day to 29 December.

At the first closing date

Once the deadline set out in the offer document, which must be at least 21 days following the date on which the offer document is posted, has passed, the board of the offeree needs to compare the position reached on each point with the conditions precedent set out in the offer. The secretary will prepare an analysis for the board (or a committee thereof) of the conditions precedent and the extent to which each has been fulfilled or not. If all conditions have been fulfilled, then the offer is declared wholly unconditional. If not, the offer may be withdrawn, may be extended or may be declared unconditional as to acceptances.

As part of the analysis of conditions precedent, totals of complete and incomplete acceptances should be finalised for consideration by the board of the offeror (or a committee thereof). The Panel issues a Receiving Agents' Code of Practice covering the problem areas which can arise in calculating the level of valid acceptances received. The details of these procedures will change considerably once CREST is fully operational for either bidder or target but the principles and legal framework will not change. The board decides whether the acceptances received to date are sufficient in number to justify declaring the offer unconditional or whether an announcement should be made of the extension of the period for acceptances before the offer becomes or is declared unconditional.

To decide whether or not to declare the offer unconditional as to acceptances the board needs both the number of acceptances and also the terms of the relevant condition in the offer document. This will usually read something similar to:

> The Offer is conditional, *inter alia*, upon:
> valid acceptances being received not later that 3.00 pm on [date] (or such later date(s) as Bidco may decide) in respect of not less than 90 per cent of the Targetco shares to which the Offer relates (or such lesser percentage (carrying more than 50 per cent of the votes) as Bidco may decide).

In this case the declaration cannot be made before the 50 per cent threshold is reached. After the 50 per cent threshold has been achieved but before it has 90 per cent acceptances the bidder is free under the terms of this sample condition to declare the offer unconditional as to acceptances at any particular time and at any particular level. To comply with the City Code, this decision should be made within 60 days of the posting of the offer document. In making this decision, there are several factors to bear in mind. These include:

- only if the target becomes a 51 per cent subsidiary will it be a member of the bidder's 'group' for group income purposes and for the purpose of surrendering ACT. It will then also become eligible to be a member of the bidder's group for VAT purposes;
- only if the target becomes a 75 per cent subsidiary will it be a member of the bidder's group for group relief purposes and for the purposes of gaining exemption from capital gains tax on intra-group transfers;
- only if the bidder obtains 75 per cent of the voting rights of the target will it be certain that it could ensure that special and extraordinary resolutions are passed;
- inter-group transfer stamp duty relief will only be available if the bidder acquires 90 per cent of the total issued share capital of the target; and
- it is not possible to acquire a minority compulsorily under sections 428–430 of the Companies Act 1985 when less than 90 per cent of the shares bid for have been acquired.

It should be noted that legislation can change these factors and that the tax definitions particularly should be checked by an expert before the board makes its decision.

Generally once an offer has been declared unconditional as to acceptances then the 90 per cent level is achieved shortly thereafter. There have been few instances where an offer has been declared unconditional at less than 90 per cent acceptances and the bidder has not subsequently been able to implement the compulsory purchases provisions. To do so the 90 per cent level may be achieved at any time before four months have elapsed from the posting of the offer document. The exceptions can include the cases where just one or two shareholders account for most or all of the remaining amount. If they hate the bidder enough, they may keep their shares to make life difficult rather than realise their investment.

In considering whether to declare an offer unconditional, it must be remembered that the offer must, under rule 34 of the Code, have granted an accepting shareholder a right of withdrawal of his or her acceptance after the expiry of 21 days from the first closing date of the initial offer. This is generally 42 days after posting. These rights are important when there are competing bidders as accepting shareholders can change their minds at this stage. Withdrawal forms are commonly sent to the target company's shareholders by the competing offerors pointing out that they have a right to withdraw their acceptances of any other offeror's offer. An offeror may not require irrevocable acceptances after that date.

If it is decided to extend the offer, the next closing date must be stated in the announcement. If statements in relation to the duration of an offer such as 'the offer will not be extended beyond a specified date unless it is unconditional as to acceptances' were included in the documents sent to the offeree company shareholders, or were made by or on behalf of an offeror and not withdrawn immediately if incorrect, only in exceptional circumstances will the offeror be allowed subsequently to extend its offer beyond the stated date except where the right to do so has been specifically reserved. If it is announced that the offer will remain open until further notice, then the next closing date must be given in any extension of the offer. There is no obligation to extend an offer the conditions of which have not been met at the first or any subsequent closing date. Where the extension of an offer involves a revision to that offer, then rule 32 of the City Code lays down the terms and time limits within which action must be taken and the exceptional cases in which an offeror may change statements already made. If revised, an offer must be kept open for at least 14 days following the date on which the revised offer document is posted. So no revision can be made in the 14-day period ending on the last day the offer is able to become unconditional as to acceptances, that is more than 46 days from the original posting date. This is also the last day on which an offeror which is including a share exchange in its offer may make an announcement about its trading results, profits, dividends or assets value. This is because such an announcement may alter the value of the offeror's shares and so amount to a revision of the bid. In 1992 Greene King's offer for Morland was in the form of convertible preference shares in Greene King. Thus Greene King had to honour its earlier announcement that the offer would not be increased by delaying the announcement of its annual results and of its five-yearly asset revaluation.

If at the first or any subsequent closing date the offer is declared unconditional as to acceptances but other conditions precedent remain to be fulfilled, then an announcement to that effect must be made. After an offer has become or been declared unconditional as to acceptances, the offer must remain open for acceptance for not less than 14 days after the date on which it would otherwise have expired. Under rule 31 of the Code an offer may not become nor be declared unconditional as to acceptances after midnight on the

60th day after the day the initial offer document was posted ('the final day rule'). On that day an announcement should be made by 5.00 pm as to whether the offer is unconditional as to acceptances or has lapsed and must include a statement as to the current position in the count. In certain restricted cases with the Panel's consent this time limit can be varied. The timing of and the details to be included in any announcement of acceptance levels are set out in rule 17. Failure to comply with these requirements can invoke the suspension of the offeree company's shares and if appropriate of the offeror's shares by the Stock Exchange and gives any acceptor the right to withdraw acceptance.

All conditions must be fulfilled (or waived) or the offer must lapse within 21 days of the first closing date or of the date the offer becomes or is declared unconditional as to acceptances, whichever is later. Under rule 31.7 the Panel has power to grant extensions but has shown reluctance to do so where the problem could have been avoided by better advance planning on the part of the offeror. Some conditions may be waived by resolution of the offeror's board. However, as the most likely laggards are consents from overseas regulators, a waiver may not be a permissible choice and the need for advance planning and prompt submissions to appropriate parties must again be emphasised. Where the offer became unconditional as to acceptances on or before the first closing date, then the deadline is 'Day 42', or 42 days after posting. If, as is common when there are competing offers, an offer is not declared unconditional until Day 60, then all other conditions must be satisfied by 81 days after posting.

Settlement of consideration

When all the conditions precedent have been met or they have been either met or waived by the board of the offeror the time limits in relation to the issue of the consideration start to run. Except with the consent of the Panel, all conditions must be fulfilled or the offer must lapse within 21 days of the first closing date or of the date on which the offer becomes or is declared unconditional as to acceptances, whichever is the later. The consideration documents may be share certificates, loan notes, warrants, warrants for cash or other documents as defined in the offer document. The consideration must be posted within 21 days of the later of:

- the first closing date of the offer,
- the date the offer becomes or is declared wholly unconditional, or
- the date of receipt of an acceptance complete in all respects.

Thus where an offer becomes unconditional as to acceptances after 60 days and becomes or is declared wholly unconditional 21 days later, the consideration will not have to be posted until 102 days after the offer, the latest possible date. The bulk of the work in this respect will be carried out by the receiving bankers and the registrars. The board of the offeror will need to make allotments of the consideration securities from time to time and so will usually appoint a committee to carry out that function.

Offeree company announcements

The board of the offeree company should not, except with the consent of the Panel (which should be consulted in good time), announce trading results, profit or dividend forecasts, asset valuations or proposals for dividend payments after the 39th day following the posting of the initial offer document. Where the announcement of trading results and dividends would normally take place after the 39th day, every effort should be made to bring forward the date of the announcement. Where this is impractical and timely consultation takes place, the Panel will normally give its consent to a later announcement. In that case the Panel will normally also be prepared to grant an extension to the final day rule, except in the case of announcements of trading results and dividends in accordance with the offeree company's normal timetable which do not appear likely to influence materially the outcome of the offer.

CHAPTER 11

The extraordinary general meeting

Arrangements

Too often in recent years company chairmen have discovered that the shareholders' meetings have not been the set-piece presentations of previous years. Company general meetings once fell into one of two categories:

- the routine low-profile, non-event;
- the theatrical show by the public relations team.

There is now a third category:

- the noisy débâcle hijacked by well-prepared protestors.

Acrimonious exchanges between current and former chairmen were displayed to all shareholders present on a huge video screen at one annual general meeting at the Wembley Arena. One clearing bank chairman was doused in paint as he entered the hall to chair an annual general meeting. At another bank's general meeting irate shareholders handcuffed themselves in turn to the microphone and lectern and bolt-cutters had to be found to remove them while the business of the meeting was suspended in uproar.

An extraordinary general meeting by its very nature may be more controversial than the routine business of an annual general meeting. A successful extraordinary general meeting is an important part of the whole takeover exercise. The company secretary is responsible for ensuring that the business of the meeting is conducted properly and effectively as a matter of law. This can conflict with the ideas of event planners and public relations personnel. The company secretary will also be expected to provide an instant and smooth response to any developments during the course of the meeting. These could be protesters, unexpected motions or amendments, complaints from the floor or the demand for a poll.

These problems are exacerbated by the fact that the law applicable at company meetings is complex and thus difficult to apply. Many aspects depend on the precise wording of the company's Articles as well as legal precedent. This makes the law difficult to clarify and apply correctly in the heat of the moment as tempers rise and disorder threatens. Thorough preparation and briefing of all concerned is essential. For the chairman and the company secretary who are in the firing line on the day such preparation is imperative.

Articles of Association

Familiarity with the company's Articles of Association is essential. A significant part of the Articles is taken up with proceedings at general meetings and related matters such as voting and notices. Each company has its own specific provisions to deal with various matters. Some of these may reflect the problems of previous general meetings. An Article may allow meetings to be conducted at several venues so that overflow rooms with audio-visual links can be used if there are too many shareholders to be accommodated in the main hall. The chairman may be permitted to adjourn the meeting without the need to put the matter to the vote as normally required in certain defined circumstances where such a vote cannot be taken.

One extraordinary general meeting which tested both those points was that considered by the Court of Appeal in *Byng* v. *London Life* ([1989] 2 W.L.R. 738). London Life had booked Cinema 1 at the Barbican for its extraordinary general meeting. Shareholder approval was needed for an amendment to its memorandum of association to allow a proposed merger. Cinema 1 proved too small for all who attended and the audio-visual links to the overflow rooms did not work properly. The meeting was opened late at 12.30 pm while members were still registering to vote. After about quarter of an hour, a door to Cinema 1 was forced open letting in what was described as a 'muted roar' from the foyer. The chairman then adjourned the meeting until 2.30 pm the same day at the Café Royal. A number of members had indicated that they could not attend the reconvened meeting before the chairman declared the adjournment. The meeting at the Café Royal was attended by 600 people, less than three-quarters of the members who had registered at the Barbican. At the Café Royal, the resolution was passed on a poll.

The court decided that it was possible to hold valid meetings using overflow rooms so long as the correct steps are followed, including the provision of adequate audio-visual links. As the audio-visual links had failed to work, the only meeting was that in Cinema 1, but since members had been excluded it was not possible to transact business at that meeting. However, the meeting was capable of adjournment. The chairman had an inherent power to adjourn the meeting but he had exercised that power invalidly because he failed to take account of relevant factors. There was no absolute necessity to obtain shareholders' approval to the business – a proposed merger – until over five months after the meeting and those who could not be at the Café Royal that afternoon were not only unable to speak, but were also unable to vote, even by proxy. The Café Royal meeting and the business purportedly transacted at it were, therefore, invalid. A new extraordinary general meeting had to be convened.

If any member who is entitled to attend and wishes to do so is unable to be accommodated in the meeting room(s), the meeting is not validly held for the purpose of transacting business. However, even though the meeting is incapable of proceeding to business by reason of the exclusion of members wishing to attend, there will be a meeting which is capable of adjournment. In any circumstances where there is a meeting at which the views of the majority cannot be validly ascertained, the chairman has a residual common law power to adjourn so as to give all persons entitled to do so a reasonable opportunity to speak and vote. This residual power, which must be exercised in good faith, can only be exercised when two other conditions are satisfied:

1. the machinery provided by the articles must have broken down;
2. the power must be exercised with a view to facilitating the presence of those entitled to debate and vote on a resolution at a meeting where such debate and voting is possible.

Admission of journalists

The press are commonly admitted to general meetings. Total exclusion of the press could of itself generate further press interest and will not create goodwill with the press. However television cameras are not commonplace at general meetings and it is not a good idea to allow a camera crew in. The spectacle of an orderly meeting is unlikely to be considered newsworthy. Short clips of general mayhem and disorder can be given undue prominence, dominating news coverage with an unfairly negative image of the meeting. This does not apply to a camera under the control of the company where the company retains editorial control. Some large companies record their annual general meetings, which are then broadcast, usually in the early hours of the morning, to enable their shareholders (and any others interested) to record the broadcast and to watch the proceedings at their leisure.

Questions

Case law makes it clear that the ability of all who wish to join in the debate before a resolution is put to the vote is a key reason in law for a general meeting. Questions (and comment masquerading as question) can range from a request for a specific and relevant piece of information to the totally weird. Both can be embarrassing to those targeted and the most reasonable question is embarrassing to the unprepared. The Cadbury Report encourages companies to consider arrangements which enable shareholders to send in questions in advance. This helps the chairman to ensure that issues of concern to many people are tackled and receive a considered reply. However care is needed to make sure that debate from the floor is not stifled. Failure to allow proper debate could give rise to legal difficulties.

The chairman should be given detailed guidance on how to bring a question session to a close. It may not be possible to carry on until there are no further questions from the floor, but a refusal to allow questions could lead to accusations that the chairman is not acting impartially or within his powers. Discussion may be limited to matters directly relevant to the resolution before the meeting. The chairman could require that all debate on one particular topic be taken at one time, refusing to take questions on that particular aspect at other times. This can be an effective tactic if there is a matter of particular concern to a protest group. The rights of members to speak may be limited but in this case great care must be taken to impose the limits impartially. A chairman might allow each member only one opportunity to speak or could limit the time allowed to each speaker.

In deciding when to end the debate, the chairman should ensure that those attending the meeting feel that they have been given a fair hearing. If this is afforded to them, it will tend to limit the force of protest and to help to keep the sympathy of the meeting. 'Give him enough rope to hang himself' is a good maxim in conducting a public meeting. The majority will tire of the unreasonable, vociferous troublemaker shortly before a good chairman takes action to silence or remove the offender. Similarly, support for the closing of debate may be forthcoming if the chairman deliberately allows a few repetitive questions before observing that the topic has clearly been exhausted.

Members are entitled to attend and to speak. Proxies are entitled to attend but have no legal entitlement to speak at a general meeting of a public limited company unless the company's Articles expressly permit. This technical legal point is rarely taken in the interest of promoting debate and avoiding any impression of defensive suppression of debate. The properly appointed representative of a corporate member has the same rights to speak, to vote on a show of hands and to do anything else which the corporate member whom he or she represents could do if it were a person. The proxy for such a representative however has no more rights than any other proxy.

The chairman is not obliged to answer any question if he or she does not consider it to be in the company's interests. A plain refusal may be an unwise course and gentle deflection may be preferable. The former politicians who move on to grace the City boardrooms must have a practical advantage here! The week before the meeting will be well spent in several sessions with as wide a cross-section of interests as possible brainstorming on likely and unlikely questions and agreeing on the best answer. It will improve the interplay of the meeting and the quality of the answers if some of the questions are passed to other directors for them to reply. The chairman will, of course, be aware in advance that the director concerned is well rehearsed in the reply to the particular question. The shareholders will still find the question no one else has thought of, but the groundwork will mean that you are better placed to cope with it. The trickiest legal points of all are inevitably referred to the company secretary. After one meeting where as secretary I had dealt with such a question – the only one we had not foreseen – the shareholder concerned spoke to me afterwards: 'You did so well in responding to my question, my dear, I shall send you advance notice next time.'

Motions from the floor

The chairman must be briefed beforehand and supplied with easy-to-read notes on how to deal with the wide range of motions that may be put from the floor. What if a dissatisfied shareholder proposes the removal of the chairman as the chairman of the meeting and the appointment in his place of Mrs Black as chairman of the meeting? Is the chairman required to allow this resolution to be put? Almost certainly not. Most limited company Articles provide that the chairman, so long as he or she is present at the meeting, shall preside as chairman of the meeting. If the chairman is taken ill during the meeting and has to leave, then the provisions of the Articles must be followed. In practice, the most senior director present would adjourn the meeting briefly and then reconvene taking the chair.

Motions to amend resolutions are particularly difficult. The scope for amending special resolutions is very limited but on ordinary resolutions it can be much more difficult to determine whether an amendment is permissible. If a valid amendment is rejected and not submitted to the meeting, then the resolution actually carried will be invalidated (*Henderson* v. *Bank of Australia* (1890) 45 Ch. D 330).

When a special resolution is proposed, it cannot be amended except in very limited ways. It is a statutory requirement that at least 21 days' notice must have been given of a special resolution. 'The resolution' means the resolution actually passed and so no substantive amendment may be made. In an unreported case (*Re Fenner plc* 11 June 1990) the court held that commonsense should prevail and that an amendment should stand. The resolution was to reduce the company's share capital and set out certain numbers of shares which, by the time of the meeting, were inaccurate because of the exercise of some share options subsequent to the notice of meeting. The meeting purported to amend the figures to bring them up to date as later upheld by the court. The court was influenced by the argument that the substantive object of the resolution was to reduce the share capital by £500,000 and this remained unaltered throughout.

The following principles apply to amendments to ordinary resolutions. They:

- must be within the scope of the notice of the meeting,
- must be no more onerous on the company, and
- must not have the effect of negating the substantive resolution.

Proposed amendments can be rejected on the grounds of redundancy (seeking to reopen business already settled by the meeting), inconsistency (incompatibility with a previous decision of the meeting) or on the grounds that the proposed amendments are obstructive, vexatious, dilatory or irrelevant. These latter grounds would need careful consideration before use.

Many public companies have provisions in their Articles requiring that no amendment to the text of ordinary resolutions set out in full in the notice of meeting shall be considered, except at the discretion of the chairman, unless 48 hours' notice in writing of the proposed amendment has been given to the company. Any use of discretion by the chairman should again be impartial. If notice is given, there will be time to seek advice on whether or not the amendment is acceptable. If an amendment was expected and does not materialise within the time limit in the Articles, it would be prudent to review the legal position and then to brief the chairman on what constitutes the notice to the company in case there is any argument at the meeting over whether or not such notice was given.

Voting on amendments

A vote should first be taken on whether or not to accept the amendment. The Article referred to above only offers to consider an amendment of which proper notice is given, not to accept it as an amendment. This will be followed by a separate vote on the resolution itself – as amended, if the meeting has already voted to accept the amendment. If the amendment is accepted or rejected on a show of hands, a poll can be validly demanded at that point. The chairman is probably entitled to say whether the poll will be taken immediately, or at the end of the meeting. If the end of the meeting is chosen to avoid disruption to the business, then three polls will have to be taken at the end of the meeting:

1. a poll on whether or not to accept the amendment;
2. a poll on the resolution as proposed to be amended;
3. a poll on the original unamended resolution.

If, under the first poll, the amendment is accepted, the second poll will determine the result of the resolution and the third poll is irrelevant (and vice versa if the amendment is rejected under the first poll).

Points of order

A point of order should be dealt with in the same way as general questions put by shareholders, with the important difference that it must be dealt with immediately. A point of order arises when in the opinion of a shareholder, the rules governing the conduct of meetings are broken or where a member has a genuine doubt as to the correctness of the procedure followed. Others present should be given an opportunity to speak on a point of order if they so desire. The chairman's ruling on a point of order is final.

Voting

In a crowded and divided meeting it can be surprisingly difficult on a show of hands to judge the result, particularly on a special/extraordinary resolution where those for must exceed those against by at least 3 to 1. Arrangements should be made in advance to enable the chairman to demand a precise hand count, which may avoid the additional delay and expense of conducting a poll.

Steps should be taken to ensure that only those entitled to vote are counted. Normally this is done through the issue of colour-coded attendance cards which members raise when they vote. Arrangements for tellers to count the votes are also best made in advance.

Are you prepared for a poll?

The chairman needs to be well briefed to avoid the pitfalls involved both in demands for a poll and in conducting them. Arrangements should be made so that demands for a poll from the floor can be verified and checked quickly. Special cards should be prepared for the chairman and for any other directors who have been appointed as proxy for a number of shareholders. The scrutineers should be on hand and properly equipped. Detailed advance planning is invaluable in this minefield.

Disruptions

If debate goes beyond mere discussion then the chairman is entitled:

- to ask the disrupters in question to sit down and only to make relevant points;
- to explain to the meeting any relevant background to the disruption;
- to offer the disrupter separate discussion outside the meeting;
- to suspend proceedings (without the necessity for an adjournment) while the disturbance is dealt with;
- if disruptions continue, to ask them to leave;
- if they do not go willingly, to expel them. This should be done only with the consent of the meeting (that is, by putting the proposition to the vote) and also with the minimum of force necessary.

A brief to cover the above steps is included in the appendix. A sufficient number of stewards should be on hand for a large meeting. It is vital that they are well briefed and that they are aware of the need to use minimum effective force to avoid any claim for assault.

Change of venue

Sometimes it becomes clear, after the notice has gone out but before the day of the meeting, that the venue will definitely have to be changed. Both Commercial Union in 1992 and National Westminster in 1993 had convened their annual general meetings at venues which were subsequently devastated by bomb damage days before their respective meetings. In each case the meeting was officially declared open and declared adjourned as close to the original site as safety permitted and was then reconvened later in the day at an alternative venue. Shareholders had been alerted to the last-minute changes by newspaper advertisements. One of the companies ran its advertisement in the Sunday newspapers whose front pages carried the bomb story as headline news. That is the kind of efficiency you can achieve with careful contingency planning.

Whenever it is necessary to change the venue after notice of a meeting has been sent out but before the date set for the meeting, the proper course of action is to open the meeting at the original venue but immediately adjourn to the revised venue. The meeting can be started with the minimum number of people necessary to satisfy the quorum requirements, before reconvening a little later at the new venue. It is obviously sensible to make efforts to inform members in advance of the change of venue if at all possible. This would be by circular if there were time but for last-minute changes by newspaper and radio advertisements.

Class meetings

Occasionally, the business proposed will not only need the approval of the ordinary shareholders but also of holders of other classes of security. The general rules and recommendations for the conduct of meetings apply. It will usually be convenient to hold the meeting(s) at the same venue and date and at a time immediately following the ordinary shareholder meeting or another class meeting. Articles or other constitutional documents – trust deeds, for example – must be read with great care. The notice requirements, quorums and majorities required to pass resolutions are frequently much more onerous than those for ordinary shares. Be ready to allow an extra week's notice of meeting, or even two, and to build enough leeway into the timetable to adjourn an inquorate meeting to reconvene a week later when reduced quorum requirements may apply. As always, knowing your company's Articles and other documents pays off.

CHAPTER 12

Now it's happened

Now the target has become part of your group. The new subsidiaries, staff and businesses must be integrated into your systems. However decentralised the group, there will be group procedures to follow, reporting and authorisation rules to be introduced in the new acquisition, and matters as diverse as insider dealing rules and sponsorship to be considered. There is also that action plan drawn up in the heat of battle on the inadequate information then available to be implemented. This must be made to deliver the benefits promised in the volumes of paper dispatched to the shareholders of both companies.

Action for integration

To integrate the acquisition, a management team is needed whose members work well together and understand the culture of the new owners. Immediately an acquisition has taken place, both the buyer and the business or company acquired face great uncertainty. In most cases the head office staff of the acquired company will have left within a year. When an investment holding company buys a successful business a large proportion of the management and staff may be retained. They will still be extremely anxious in the early days and some changes are inevitable. When a business in trouble is purchased by experts in turnaround situations, then immediate and drastic changes are to be expected and will happen. If major cuts are to happen, do it fast and if possible let everyone know where they stand within a month.

In all acquisitions the holding company will impose its own performance demands and accounting methods. The extent to which the membership of the board changes will depend on the owner's culture. Some exert their powers as shareholders; others through membership of the subsidiary or divisional board, often by appointing the managing director of their choice.

A business plan has to be agreed between the head office team and the acquisition's board. This will reflect the homework done before the bid or purchase on the savings and synergies which could be achieved. Good communications by line management to staff remain most important in this phase. This is true both in the acquisition and in any divisions of the purchaser who are to work closely with the new division. Where the synergy argument leads to a full merger whether with all or part of the purchaser's business, then the planning and communication skills are crucial.

By forcing the acquired company to alter its performance measurement and reporting methods, its culture will be changed. With some carefully targeted senior management changes this can lead to dramatic improvements. If it is planned to keep the services and the industry expertise of certain existing directors, start work on building the relationships with them during the process of purchase or bid. Entrepreneurs who have built up and run their own businesses their own way may find it difficult to report to any one. Directors who have been made wealthy as a result of the sale may find that their appetite for work and their attitude to a business which is no longer their own have changed.

Expert advice is essential before taking steps to rationalise property assets, computer systems or manufacturing plant. In each case action before all aspects of the change have been considered can be costly. It may be cheaper to live with surplus space in the short term than to put it into order for a fast disposal. This can be built into an on-going review of the group's property needs. Incompatible computers have frustrated mergers and takeovers. This is especially true in businesses where the main services to customers are provided by the technology, such as building societies. Rationalisation of manufacturing plant gives handsome rewards but will always take longer than you first thought. Capital equipment takes time to move, alter or replace. Different conventions in production engineering and part numbering also take time to resolve if a satisfactory outcome is to be achieved.

The buyers will also suffer some change of culture as adjustments are made to integrate the new division into the group. A company hitherto in a specialist market may see public relations as the preserve of head office dealing with analysts and the City press and have an unwritten but well-understood rule that only the group managing director talks to the press. Acquiring a business with a much higher profile of more general interest can be a shock. Not only do routine public relations continue in the new subsidiary keeping the group in the public eye, but its staff may talk about possible changes and even write letters – anonymous or signed – to the press without any reference to 'higher authority'. A money-broker who invests in television finds that life is now lived in a goldfish bowl.

Becoming a group

One needs the basic data about what has been bought as soon as possible. In an agreed acquisition of a listed company, the first wave of enthusiasm for learning more about the 'new group member' – rather than the 'target' – had to be firmly controlled until the offer went unconditional. The City Code insists that every bidder is entitled to the same information about a target in the interests of fair play and level playing fields. So as long as another bidder might come into play, restraint was the watchword, to the frustration of the chief executive and those who masterminded the strategy of the bid.

The next stage allows information gathering and detailed planning to begin. Once the bid has 'gone unconditional' and the procedures under sections 428–430 can start (see Chapter 13), we need to know as much as possible about our new toy and to find out whether we can really achieve the savings, new markets, economies of scale, synergies, etc. that were promised to the shareholders.

There remains a constraint on implementing certain actions at this stage of play. Until the section 428 procedure is complete, the only changes which can be made are those within the powers of the board without reference to shareholders. Any legal restructuring of the group, for example for tax efficiency, will probably have to wait also until the companies to be moved are wholly owned.

First, this avoids any problems of consent. Second, it avoids spending time checking whether certain tax planning arrangements will work for partly owned undertakings. Third, at least for companies registered in the United Kingdom, relief from stamp duty on the transfer of shares may be claimed under section 42 of the Finance Act 1930 as amended by section 27 of the Finance Act 1967 where the degree of association is that one body corporate be the beneficial owner of not less that 90 per cent of the issued share capital of the other. The relationship can exist through complex family trees as set out in part 1 of the 4th Schedule of the Finance Act 1938. The claim must be adjudicated under the provisions of section 12 of the Stamp Act 1891. Clearly, some parts of the law with which we must deal are more enduring than others.

In law, such a claim can be made as soon as the buyer is in a position to comply with the requirements of section 429, but in practice the statutory declaration which must be sworn by 'a responsible officer of the parent body corporate' is much more easily prepared once the dissenters have been removed from the share register. A responsible officer for this purpose is a person who has the right and duty to attend all board meetings where policy is decided and who is, therefore, aware of the parent company's future policy concerning the subsidiary and its assets. This statutory declaration needs full details of the bodies corporate concerned and of all companies in the family tree through which the relationship is established:

- date of incorporation,
- registered number,
- authorised capital,
- issued capital,
- number of shares held by the parent,
- number of shares held by a nominee of the parent.

Getting the information

In this section, we confine ourselves to the information needed by the company secretary responsible for group compliance. It might be assumed that this is a simple matter. Visit the company secretary of the newly acquired group, introduce yourself and your group procedures and wire their computers into your group's e-mail and company secretarial software.

It does not work like that in real life. Meet each other, yes. You will probably already have met across a table during the negotiations or the late-night sessions completing documents. Then you were both literally and figuratively on opposite sides of the table. So if the game plan requires a continuing relationship, try to arrange the first meeting on neutral territory so that you can establish some rapport without that table between you. Otherwise, visit the new location and start learning how the new acquisition ticks – even if the tempo is about to undergo a major change.

It is much more likely that the game plan sees a future for only one PLC-level secretary in the group. In which case these initial contacts will be less amicable, especially if you suspect that someone else's game plan says, 'Let's run with them both for a couple of months and then decide who's to get the job.' If that is the culture of the company you live in, then you probably have the political skills needed to survive without my help.

My lucky break was finding myself just three months into a new post working on a merger. Our company was quoted on the Unlisted Securities Market and the other had a full Stock Exchange listing, so the deal was structured as an acquisition of my employer by the listed company. I very quickly signed my service contract which contained a three months' notice clause and forgot all the minor queries I had been negotiating on it! The secretary of the acquiring company had been an active participant in all negotiations and was also one of the continuing executive directors, so my concern about the future was great. We met as soon as the shareholders had approved the deal. Within minutes, I learned that as finance director and company secretary combined he was overstretched and had got his board's authority to recruit a chartered secretary for the role. However, the deal had come up and he had not had time to start the recruitment process. We rapidly converted the authorisation to recruit into that for a professional assistant for me and I attended and minuted the first board meeting of the enlarged company, minuting my own appointment. So having joined a USM company in November, I found myself by April the secretary of a listed company of twice the size which became much better known than either of its constituent parts had been.

Whatever the personal circumstances, it is necessary to establish contact with the person responsible for statutory records and compliance in the new subsidiary, then to identify what data are held by them, in what form and to what extent matters are subcontracted. The newly acquired group may have a centralised in-house database at one extreme. At the other, it may be a minimal head office with all divisional matters dealt with at a divisional level – common where a company frequently buys and sells its subsidiaries and sees them as investments providing a return on capital rather than as integral parts of a group. It may outsource all its work. There are public limited companies where the company secretary with a shared member of the support staff manages the outsources and participates in the running of the board's meetings; everything else is handled by outside specialists. There are as many variations on the theme as there are groups of companies. So be prepared for the unexpected.

You will want to know about all the areas of your direct responsibility. These are likely to include:

- statutory records for the UK companies,
- statutory records for overseas,
- registration,
- dissenters' records from earlier acquisitions,
- share options – executive,
- share options – sharesave,
- share options – any unusual schemes,
- other share-based benefits,
- profit-sharing schemes,
- personnel responsibilities,
- pension arrangements,
- insurance cover,
- risk management,
- storage of contracts and documents of title,
- information databases,
- lawyers and matters outsourced to them,
- insider dealing rules and records,
- litigation in progress,
- intellectual property,
- facilities management and property records,
- corporate governance procedures,
- delegated authorities,
- public relations,
- annual reports,
  and also:
- what have I not thought of?

The answers to many questions may show that the group used certain functions for certain responsibilities. However, the very last is likely to produce the most unexpected answers of all. So often, those who have worked in a company for a long time carry the baggage of sundry tasks with them from job to job.

New subsidiaries

The company secretarial database needs rapid updating. If you are lucky, the new arrivals had a central database on the same software as yours. If you were wise at purchase time, your software can import information from a compatible database, that is transfer the information electronically. If appropriate the head office of the new division can continue to maintain its records locally but network them to your machine so that the group database is always current. If less lucky, the computer boffins scratch their heads over file incompatibility and work overtime, or you hire a temporary input person to crunch the new data into your system. If you are unlucky, their records are manual and in a mess. Then one of your brightest assistants is tied up in detective work in dusty files for far too long, or you contract out the work to a chartered secretary in practice.

Whatever the position, do not put off tackling the task. Sooner rather than later someone will need the data urgently. The data will already be changing fast. New directors will have been appointed to the acquired company and some of its key subsidiaries. If the lawyers change and their office was the registered address, you want to be able to generate the relevant minutes and forms 287 on your computer; not to have to type them and re-input the details later. Form 287 must be used to give notice of a change of registered address to the Registrar of Companies. The change only takes effect when Form 287 has been placed on the register at Companies House, that is has literally become the 'registered address'. Other directors will leave and accounting reference dates may need to change. A subsidiary must transfer to within the original group and a statutory declaration claiming relief from stamp duty needs to be prepared as explained earlier. Get the data organised and the standard procedures in place. As most secretarial procedures are heavily influenced by the requirements of the Companies Acts this is one field of operation where adaptation to a new owner is unlikely to be traumatic.

Tax advisers appear

In any group a major change in structure provides opportunities for tax planning; so do possible changes in accounting dates. In an international organisation these are multiplied dramatically. Companies may be moved; trades may be moved. Companies surplus to operating requirements may need to stay in business to use existing losses or provide ACT relief. The secretaries must ensure that in executing these proposals the proper forms are observed. Each company's directors must act in the best interests of that company and must declare their interests in any other group company involved in the transaction under consideration. Board meetings, duly minuted, must take decisions for each company concerned. Where necessary, minutes must take place in the correct timed sequence. For clarity it is possible to record a telephone board meeting as taking place at '10.00 am UK time, 11.00 am Netherlands time' and to evidence it by a facsimile transmission of a document to be seen or signed by all parties present.

The tax department and the outside advisers will be among the first customers for your expanded database on the new group structure. They will continue to be so and will expect your help in ensuring that section 179 of the Taxation of Chargeable Gains Act 1992 is not forgotten. This section provides that if a company ceases to be a member of a group holding an asset which it acquired on an intra-group transfer within the previous six years, then that company is deemed for tax purposes to have sold and reacquired that asset at market value at the time of the original intra-group transfer. Even in the simplest acquisition this has serious implications for the purchaser since it is the acquired company which is liable to pay the tax. While impractical in an open market bid, in a private acquisition a careful investigation needs to be made of any assets held in the target company which might be the subject of a section 179 charge on completion of the transaction. In such cases suitable warranties and indemnities should be negotiated. However, it is worth enquiring if substantial liabilities are known to exist and if so to take particular account of them, perhaps through an adjustment in the purchase price.

If the vendor has engaged in tax planning prior to the sale, then it is likely that a number of intra-group transfers will have occurred and moreover a number more may be necessary in order to effect a sensible post-acquisition reorganisation. In these circumstances, almost inevitable in a public bid, a careful note of the movement of all significant companies around a sub-group needs to be kept in order that capital gains tax liabilities are not triggered accidentally in future. It may be helpful to have a note prepared by the purchaser's lawyers to the board of directors to provide a 'bible' for the six years following any post-acquisition reorganisation. This would cover transactions which should not be undertaken or which need to be undertaken only in a specific way to avoid triggering a tax charge.

Accounting reference dates

There is a natural desire to align the acquisition's accounting year with that of its new parent as soon as possible. However, first check the position with the tax advisers and learn when would be the optimum point at which to make the change. The rules for changes to accounting reference dates are set out in the Companies Act 1985, sections 224–226, as amended by the Companies Act 1989. Before making a change in the date you need to know whether the notice is being given during the first nine months following incorporation, during the accounting reference period to be altered or after the end of the period to be altered. The last case is only permitted if the company is a subsidiary coming into line with its parent or in administration. It should be noted that companies in a group which do not fit the Companies Act definition of a subsidiary undertaking are excluded from making the change after the end of the accounting period in question. It is also necessary to decide whether to shorten or extend the accounting reference period being changed. The same exceptions apply if an extension is required within five years of the end of an accounting reference period which was extended.

When the period is shortened then the time allowed for laying and delivering accounts for the period is set out in Companies Act 1985, section 242(5). Diary notes should be made to ensure these limits are observed.

New directors

Any new members of the main board should be provided with similar information packs to those provided to any new director. If the director is not already a director of a listed company, then the declaration for new directors should be filed with the Securities & Futures Authority. Otherwise the other company, the SFA or the Stock Exchange should be asked to confirm the date on which a declaration was filed. A diary note should be made to remind the secretary when the next triennial filing is due.

CHAPTER 13

The aftermath

Dissenters

Whether you call them dissenters, dissenting shareholders or dissentients these people require time and attention almost as tiresome as their tongue-twisting appellation.

Those who truly dissented from the offer will respond quickly once matters have gone beyond the point of no return. Those who are knowledgeable enough or sophisticated enough to have reached their own conclusions and to decide that the price was too low or that they disliked or distrusted the proposed new owners or that their own business would be affected by the reduction in competition are not a nuisance. These shareholders have a right to their views; all the more so as they have been prepared 'to put their money where their mouth is'. Such people will be aware of press comment and screen information about the progress of an offer. They will not want their assets tied up in trusteeship and will take action once it is clear that their preferred option is not available. Other deliberate dissenters may include those who wish to delay crystallising a taxable gain into another tax year. Trustees who are uncertain of their powers of investment may wait until the holdings are compulsorily acquired rather than take action on their own initiative. This category often includes the target company as trustee for dissenters from earlier offers.

However, the majority of the so-called dissenters are really the 'don't knows' or the 'don't cares'. Many were too busy to study the volumes of information sent to them at great trouble and expense and used the 'round filing cabinet'. Others were overseas on business trips, archaeological digs or trekking holidays and missed the deadlines. Most of these surface within the year. Some catch up with their mail; others find time to read the slimmer documents arriving in the section 429 procedure. The rest are asked by their accountants at tax return time either about a dividend apparently missing or the asset which is recognised as having been subject to takeover and so capital gains tax implications arise.

The remainder contribute to the billions of pounds worth of assets lying unclaimed around the country. They have moved without forwarding addresses, refused to give their nominee discretion but then failed to give instructions, become senile, only held one share to get your paperwork or cause trouble at an annual general meeting and find accepting not worth the time or have died without leaving proper records of their assets. In one deal a nominee holding 400,000 shares without discretion confessed that those shares (worth £6.50 each!) were only a small part of the customer's assets. At a time of takeover fever he was frustrated that he could not manage the assets properly but could not get her to respond to requests for instructions! Letters were returned marked 'gone away' and her telephone number was unobtainable.

That level of value is uncommon but not rare. This rump of those who dissent through total apathy must have their interests looked after by a trustee until they claim their rights – if ever. Most commonly, these claims come when the bureau or desk has been checked by an executor or by a caring relative or friend at the time of a move into a nursing home. I once received six separate letters posted individually from a solicitor in the Shetland Islands. They were all addressed to me but in my capacity as the secretary of six different companies within the same group. On investigation, it was found that a recently deceased Shetland Islander held £78 and some unclaimed dividends where a holding of just 12 shares had been subject to an offer for cash.

So, we have a new owner who has control but not yet all the shares and some hundreds of shareholders who have already demonstrated their inability to reply to correspondence. What do we do? As always, turn to the Companies Acts.

Procedures under sections 428–430

Sections 428–430 of the Companies Act 1985 (the Act) provided compulsory acquisition procedures. These applied once an offer had become unconditional in all respects and the acquiring company owned 90 per cent or more ('not less than nine-tenths in value of the shares to which the offer relates'). It should be noted that 'the shares to which the offer relates' exclude the shares already owned by the offeror and those which it had contracted to acquire at the date of the offer and so these shares, if any, should be excluded from the calculation. These provisions were repealed with effect from 30 April 1987 by section 172 of the Financial Services Act 1986 (FSA), which substitutes new sections 428–430 contained in Schedule 12 of the FSA. Under the original Act the company which had acquired 90 per cent of the shares of another company could compulsorily acquire the dissenters' shares unless a successful application was made to the court to prevent this. On the other hand, the remaining minority could require that they be bought out. The replacement sections aim to protect the minority rights and to ensure that they are treated no less fairly than the shareholders who have accepted the offer.

An acquiring company has two months from the date the 90 per cent test is satisfied to give notices in the required form to the non-assenting shareholders in the target company. It is strongly recommended to get the notices out promptly. If not, the provisions of section 430A of the Act come into action. Section 430A carries criminal penalties for non-compliance and provides a procedure whereby the non-assenting target shareholders can oblige the acquiring company to buy their shares. No such notice is required if the section 429 notice is sent out within one month of the 90 per cent test being satisfied; this is a further reason for prompt action.

As the offer will remain open for acceptance during the period following the giving of the section 429 notice, shareholders during this time can still accept in the normal way and receive the consideration directly. Those who respond to the section 429 notice and do not formally accept the offer have to wait to the end of the six-week period to receive the consideration for their compulsorily acquired shares from the trustee for the non-assenting shareholders. An example of a typical 'back end' timetable is included in the appendix.

The notice must be given in the prescribed form and must reflect the choice of consideration under the original offer, with a separate one sent to each of any joint holders individually. It must also state the position in default of a choice (which does not necessarily have to be the basic form of the original offer). The law states that each notice should be signed by a director or the secretary of the acquiring company. Faced with having to sign by hand several hundred or more notices, this is one task the directors delegate with alacrity to the secretary! Legal advisers insist that actual signatures are required. Notices must be sent by recorded delivery within the United Kingdom and by airmail elsewhere.

The Act specifies that a copy of 'the first notice' given is to be sent to the offeree company with a statutory declaration signed by a director of the acquiring company stating that the conditions for the giving of the notice to the non-assenting shareholders are satisfied – this is one task that the directors cannot delegate to the secretary! Just as well, as making such a declaration knowing it to be false or failing to send a copy of the first notice and the statutory declaration carries a penalty of fines and/or imprisonment. To avoid question, it is worth asking the receiving bankers to agree which of the target's shareholders is to be the recipient of 'the first notice'. In addition, they must keep copies of all the notices.

Assuming that no dissenter exercises their right to make an application to the court, then six weeks after sending the notices, the acquiring company must:

- send the target company copies of each notice sent;
- pass the consideration for the shares to which the notice applies to the target to hold in trust for the relevant dissenters;
- deliver transfers for the target shares compulsorily acquired.

If very few are involved, then each stock transfer can be prepared and the following statement should appear with the signature: 'The person appointed by _____ PLC to execute this transfer in accordance with section 430(6) of the Companies Act 1985.' More usually, a block transfer is used.

If the target is a public limited company, or a limited company whose Articles require it to have two shareholders or a general meeting quorum of two, then either at the transfer stage or immediately afterwards the usual arrangements for a nominee holder and declaration of trust with blank stock transfer form should be put in place. It is possible to convert a public limited company to a private company and to change the Articles to permit a single member company. Time is unlikely to permit this luxury as almost certainly there will be matters to be dealt with in the short term which can most easily be handled by an extraordinary general meeting. It is also important to check when the annual general meetings of newly acquired companies and their annual returns are due. These mundane matters are easily overlooked under pressure of other work. And of course, the acquirer's reminder systems and computerised statutory records will not yet include the new group companies. So set up the nominee to regularise the position immediately.

The target company's response

On receipt of the stock transfers for the dissenters' shares, the target must register the bidder as the holder of those shares in the target, save possibly where requested for the one nominee. The consideration received by the target from the bidder has to be held on trust for the non-assenting former target shareholders. The target has to open a separate bank account for any cash consideration and any dividend or other monies accruing from any consideration in securities. This bank account must bear interest at an appropriate rate and allow funds to be withdrawn with appropriate notice. Any securities in the bidder will be registered in the target's name notwithstanding that it is now a subsidiary of the bidder.

Any dissenters who contact the bidder, its registrars or the receiving bankers should be paid the consideration due subject to the bidder being satisfied that they are so entitled. Entitlement is usually proven by the delivery of a share certificate(s) in the target or an indemnity where the certificates are unavailable. The legislation provides that reasonable enquiries must be made at intervals to find the dissenters entitled to distribution of the consideration. The target company should write to the dissenters once the compulsory acquisition process is complete advising them of that fact and inviting them to apply for the transfer to them of the consideration. Where the dissenters entitled to the consideration held on trust cannot be found in spite of reasonable enquiries from time to time, then after 12 years or when the target company is wound up the consideration (together with any interest, dividends or other benefits which may have accrued from it) is paid into court. The consideration never reverts to either company.

The Stock Exchange will have noted the announcement of the despatch of the section 429 notices. Once the six weeks are up (providing that no application is made to the court) the bidder will advise the Exchange that it has acquired 100 per cent ownership of the target. At that point but not before, the target's shares are removed from the Official List. If annual accounts or other actions requiring publication or announcement arise up to that point then the Continuing Obligations under the Listing Rules should be obeyed. In practice the Stock Exchange takes a fairly relaxed view about compliance with the regulations during the six-week period following the despatch of the section 429 notices.

Sale of fractions

Where new securities have been issued either as consideration for a bid or by way of a rights issue, the arithmetic frequently results in fractions of the new securities apparently due for allotment. The terms of the offer will generally state that the fractions of the new securities will not be allotted or issued to accepting shareholders. Fractional entitlements to securities are aggregated and sold in the market. The sale can be arranged by the registrars, the receiving bankers, the company or the stockbrokers. The secretary should clarify in advance who is making the sale and ensure that clear instructions are issued. For a small number, no one wants the bother. On a large number everyone volunteers to earn the commission. Just make sure the responsibility is clear; I once found the stockbroker about to sell the 33 shares arising on a conversion having already received a copy of the sale contract from the registrars. Proceeds of the sale are then distributed pro rata to those entitled, subject to a *de minimis* level below which proceeds are retained for the benefit of the company.

In the case of a rights issue the Stock Exchange requires that shares not subscribed for by existing shareholders or those to whom they have sold their rights (that is the provisional allottees) be sold for the benefit of such persons. Where the amount to which the shareholder is entitled is small, the terms of the offer may allow the proceeds of the sale to be retained for the benefit of the company.

Central Statistical Office

The Central Statistical Office compiles statistics of acquisitions and mergers made by UK industrial and commercial companies and, for the purpose, relies on inquiries to companies to confirm the details reported in the press. As soon as a takeover or merger is reported, the CSO will write to the bidder asking it to confirm whether the acquisition has taken place and seeking certain information about it. The letter, which is followed by regular reminders, is easily buried in a pending tray in the case of a public bid arriving as it does at the height of the work to get the documents despatched long before the acquisition is completed. This point when the compulsory acquisition procedure is completed is the point at which to find it and to reply. Of course, for many takeovers the matter is completed at around the time that the first announcement is made, and in those cases the CSO letter can be dealt with much more promptly.

The Central Statistical Office needs to know:

- the names of: the acquiring company,
                the acquired company,
                the vendor company;
- the date of the transaction;
- the total consideration paid for the acquisition in terms of:
                cash,
                value of ordinary shares,
                value of other securities.

The information is used to compile:

- a quarterly CSO bulletin providing data on acquisitions and mergers by industrial and commercial companies within the UK;
- an indication of the level of acquisitions and mergers activity in the United Kingdom;
- an estimate of the industrial and commercial companies' transactions in UK company securities and hence total company financing, which forms part of the financial statistics needed by the government for its assessment of economic developments and for economic planning.

Share option schemes

In most cases, the takeover provision in the scheme rules will have triggered exercises – in spite of tax penalties in many cases – and there may be no options left outstanding. That is not the end of the matter. Even if all have been exercised or lapsed, records of directors' interests (not forgetting all the companies in the group) and records of each scheme must be preserved. There will be a tax return to complete the following April. Even in an unapproved scheme there is an obligation under section 136(6) of the Income and Corporation Taxes Act 1988 to notify the Inland Revenue of events relating to options over a company's shares which may give rise to an income tax charge for an individual. Then, during the summer, there will be a fresh wave of questions from the individuals themselves or their accountants as personal tax returns are completed. Finally, after the last box of records has gone to the archive, someone will have an esoteric query from a tardy tax inspector to be answered.

In those cases where the scheme continues in existence active record-keeping continues. As will the need for regular valuations of the company whose shares are the subject of the options. Check both the rules and Articles of Association for methods of valuation, buy-back provisions, cash alternatives, restrictions on transfers of business and any other special conditions. In some cases these may be found in, or amended by, joint venture or shareholders' agreements.

Where the original share options are replaced by options over shares in the new holding company, careful reading of all the relevant rules is essential. In particular, the limits on levels of grant must be carefully reviewed and the methods of calculation identified and checked. In most such cases, the promise to 'exchange' is a goodwill offer during the earlier negotiations and a certain amount of flexibility to cope with the reality is available.

The existing option schemes of the acquirer also need review. If new shares have been issued, rules must be checked for each scheme to see whether or not options already in existence have been altered or limits changed. Generally, only the issue of new ordinary shares triggers these changes but there are exceptions. Where an event has included a rights issue or scrip issue involving ordinary shares, then changes are inevitable. Usually the scheme rules require the directors to make the changes subject to checking by the company's auditors.

Profit-sharing schemes

Shares already issued to or purchased by the trustee to the target's profit sharing scheme will have been dealt with under the acquisition procedures. It is worth pushing the trustee to produce the revised paperwork promptly. This is good for employee relations and essential for directors' interests registers. A director's position must be identified quickly to comply with the law and Yellow Book rules. Bad feeling results when staff who have not yet received details of their own entitlements read of a director's in the annual report or in an announcement of directors' dealings.

The scheme must continue as long as the trustee holds shares for members – which could be for up to five years. Thereafter, it may be closed in accordance with the terms of its own trust deed – generally by resolution of the company concerned. Like trusteeship for dissenters, this is a matter which must be recorded on that company's information sheet. The company concerned must not be sold outside the enlarged group nor dissolved nor struck off without appropriate arrangements being made.

Employee share option plan trusts

The trustee will have taken advice from any beneficial owners of the shares in their custody as to how to respond to the bid. For any shares held at the company's request the recommendations of the directors will have informed the trustees' decision. As a result, the trustees will probably hold either cash or securities in the bidder. They may also be the owners of some of the shares held by the trustee for the dissenters. The exact responsibilities of the trustee to an employee share option trust in a case where the best interests of the employees who are the beneficiaries of the trust are not necessarily the same as those of the generality of shareholders has yet to be tested in court. I know more than one lawyer who would enjoy representing the trustees in a case to resolve that conundrum.

Insider dealing rules

Insider dealing is a matter of increasing prominence and concern today. If the newly acquired company was a private one, action is simple. The staff to be treated as insiders are identified in line with the group's usual rules and the need for the rules explained. Then the insider dealing rules are issued and signed copies returned and filed in line with the standard procedures. The appropriate staff must be briefed to ensure that future recruits and promotions are also dealt with in the normal way.

Where both parties to a takeover or merger were quoted companies, relevant personnel will already be subject to their own rules. Either the ultimate holding company's rules should be quickly circulated to all concerned for consideration, signature and return, or an amendment to their current commitment pointing out that these rules now apply to dealings in the ultimate holding company's securities should be issued. The former procedure is to be preferred except when it is known that the rules will shortly change. This could be because of a change in accounting date or an imminent change in the law or the Model Code.

It is also important to identify the location of existing records of agreement to the new group member's dealing rules and of authorisations to deal. Many corporate actions are preceded by dealings which trigger the Stock Exchange's investigative powers and such records may be needed to answer enquiries.

More queries

Dissenting shareholders by definition are slow to respond. The need will depend on the size of the company's share register and the number of individual shareholders among the dissenters, but plans must remain in place for dealing with queries at both parties' premises as well at both registrars. If two major utilities merge, this may mean keeping a special helpline open for a year or more. In other cases, it may just mean a note to any temporary switchboard operators that enquiries about shares are transferred to the company secretary at head office.

New classes of stocks and shares

The terms of the new securities will have been thrashed out at length in some of the very long meetings before the deal was agreed. There will have been good reasons for choosing a particular type of security. Those involved will remember if dividends are deferred or if shares are convertible or if the loan stock carries an unusual rate of interest.

There are many people who now have to take action who were not so involved in the original drafting. There are many clauses which came straight from the lawyers' precedents and word processors with minimal attention to how they will work in practice. So *read* the documents concerned – Articles of Association, trust deeds or shareholders' agreements. When there are shareholders' agreements, watch especially for the interaction of that document with the Articles of Association and with statute. Amendments to shareholders' agreements need to be treated with even more respect. A good company secretary will identify the places where such interaction may cause a problem or produce an unexpected result before the event occurs. They are then in a position to draw the point to the executives' or board's attention in a timely fashion. The matter may still cause aggravation but can at least be tackled sensibly with advance warning.

Terms for payment of dividends or interest must be studied and the relevant accounting and treasury personnel properly briefed. Very often payment dates will reflect the fiscal year of the target and not that of the company now paying. The first payment is almost always for an odd number of days. Make sure that you have written evidence of the date from which the calculation is to run. If the security is listed, ensure that the Stock Exchange is advised of the payment date in good time. While admitting that it should be clear from documents already submitted to them, those who mark shares 'ex div' are wont to miss the approach of the first payment. Your registrars will appreciate action to make sure that the shares go ex div in sufficient time to allow them to process the dividend or interest warrants in an orderly fashion. Registrars can sometimes work miracles but it is kinder to avoid the necessity.

An over-enthusiastic registrar once sent me a dividend calculation with nine different rates of payment based on the dates on which the convertible preference shares had been allotted. She could have saved herself a lot of arithmetic by reading the Article which said: '. . . paid on a *pro rata* basis in respect of the period from the date falling 21 days after the date on which the Offer becomes or is declared unconditional in all respects . . .' The letter was so confident about the need for multiple rates that I asked the solicitor to confirm that I was not misreading or misunderstanding the Article in question.

On the same offer but in connection with the loan stock issued, the bank required to supply the interest rate misquoted. Neither our assistant treasurer's letter of request nor their response quoted the definition used in full. Interest rates had been moving about and the request was only submitted a month before the payment was due and some time after the trigger date. Thus the first person to notice that the incorrect rate had been quoted and used was the largest holder of the loan stock, also an important supplier to the new subsidiary. In that case there was an underpayment so it was relatively easy although embarrassing to send out a top-up cheque including a payment in lieu of any interest lost.

On an earlier occasion, due to a confusion over net of tax and gross payments, the warrants issued had overpaid loan stock holders. The dozen largest holders offered to return their warrants for cancellation provided that we delivered town-clearing cheques to them for the correct amounts by 2.00 pm that day. This we achieved; the registrars who were at fault grovelled in suitable fashion and we agreed to adjust the rest of the overpayments six months later. Then several minor loan stock holders who had not yet got round to banking their warrants heard that some had been returned to us and did likewise, demanding correct replacements and interest compensation. These requests were almost more difficult to deal with than the original mistake.

The next point to watch is the timing and terms of any repayment or conversion. Make sure these are built into reminder calendars, forecasting models and planning arrangements. Is there a requirement to notify shareholders of the opportunity to convert? If so, a suitable notice or letter is needed. To write it to inform without encouraging within the terms of the Financial Services Act 1986 is a major challenge. The mere receipt of the letter by the securities holders is enough to trigger at least some conversions, however disadvantageous.

For loan stock repayments, it is worth knowing that these can be delayed by changing the trust deed. It is not often done, but the holders are sometimes active participants in the business. Someone may have planned to retire early and to live abroad for a couple of years to cash in. If she or he now wishes to continue to contribute and so does the company, the term of the trust deed can be extended and the final loan repayment date delayed with the consent of the company and a majority of the loan stock holders in a class meeting.

Purchase of own shares

When a company has purchased its own shares, it must file with the Registrar of Companies on form 169 a return stating with respect to shares of each class purchased the number and nominal value of the shares and the date on which they were delivered to the company within 28 days of that date. This return must be accompanied by a remittance for stamp duty on the purchase price (Companies Act 1985, section 169; and Finance Act 1986, section 66).

The company must keep a copy of any contract to purchase its own shares at its registered office from its conclusion, that is the date on which the purchase of all the shares under the contract was completed, for a period of ten years. This copy, including any variation of it, or a memorandum of the terms if it was not in writing, is open to inspection by any member of the company and if a public company by any member of the public, without charge during normal business hours subject to reasonable restrictions.

Annual report

All changes in a company's share capital must be disclosed in the directors' report and financial statements for the year in question. Full details are set out in the Companies Act 1985, Schedule 4, paragraph 39. Chapter 12 of the Yellow Book requires certain additional disclosures to be made where allotments for cash of equity securities were made during the period under review otherwise than to the holders of the company's equity share capital in proportion to their holdings of equity shares (in other words, a rights issue) and which has not been specifically authorised by the company's shareholders. These additional disclosures are:

● the names of the allottees if less than six in number and in the case of six or more allottees a brief generic description of them;

● the market price of the securities concerned on a named date, being the date on which the terms of the issue were fixed;

● similar information must be given for the allotment of shares to third parties in any unlisted major subsidiary undertaking including the information required by Companies Act 1985, Schedule 4, paragraph 39 as if the major subsidiary undertaking were 'the company' for the purposes of that paragraph;

● where a listed company is the subsidiary undertaking of another company, particulars of the participation by the parent undertaking in any placing made during the period under review;

● particulars of any contract of significance as defined in Chapter 12 subsisting during the period to which the company or one of its subsidiaries is a party and in which a director of the company is or was materially interested or, if there has been no such contract, disclosure of that fact;

● particulars of any contract of significance, that is one where the value is 1 per cent or more of the relevant group basis, between the company or one of its subsidiaries by a controlling shareholder subsisting during the period under review;

● particulars of any contract for the provision of services to the company or any of its subsidiaries by a controlling shareholder during the period under review;

● details of small related party transactions as required by paragraph 11.8 (c) of the Yellow Book.

CHAPTER 14

Looking back

When the acquisition has become a permanent part of your business, questions may be asked about its success. Was the company right to put its funds and efforts into buying another business, or would it have been better to build organically on its existing base? In order to answer such questions, results are needed. So how do we account for acquisitions?

Acquisition accounting

There have been two different methods of accounting used in recent years where two companies (or groups) combine into a group consisting of a holding company and subsidiaries. These are acquisition accounting and merger accounting. Acquisition accounting uses the same basic principles for a share purchase as for any other asset purchase. The shares are recorded in the books of the holding company at the cost at the time of acquisition. Reasonably, this cost is deemed to include the profits made by the target company up to the date of purchase, the pre-acquisition profits. Only profits made after the purchase, the post-acquisition profits, may be reflected in the consolidated profit and loss account of the enlarged group. Only these latter profits are included in the distributable reserves of the holding company and thus only they, and not the pre-acquisition profits, may be distributed as dividends.

When a company is purchased, fair values have to be attributed to the assets and liabilities acquired. Under FRS 7 the fair values should reflect the circumstances at the time of acquisition and should not reflect either the acquirer's intentions or events subsequent to the acquisition. There are specific rules on how fair values should be determined for the main categories of assets and liabilities. The underlying principle is that fair value should reflect the price at which an asset or liability could be exchanged in an arm's length transaction. These values do not have to be reflected in the books of the subsidiary acquired but if not must be adjusted on consolidation. This includes any resulting adjustments, such as depreciation on revalued assets.

In the past, acquisition accounting has been a fruitful source of creativity. Terry Smith in *Accounting for Growth* sets out several of the more notable examples. He points out that companies have been known to make provisions for everything which can be imagined and then to make further provisions in subsequent years. While a company making an acquisition cannot always be expected to have available all the information needed to compute the fair value immediately, especially in the case of a hostile bid, there should be a limit on the extent of hindsight allowed. Clearly, the more provisions which can be made on acquisition, the healthier the accounts can look in later years. FRS 7 now addresses these abuses by excluding provisions for reorganisation costs to be carried out by the acquirer and provisions for future losses. Such items now have to be treated as part of the post-acquisition results of the enlarged group. The standard also sets out how the value attributed to the consideration should be determined and which acquisition expenses may be included in the cost of the investment.

The difference between the fair value of the consideration paid and the net of the fair values of the assets and liabilities acquired forms a premium or discount on acquisition which is shown as 'goodwill arising on consolidation' in the consolidated balance sheet. A discount or negative goodwill figure has to be written off directly to reserves immediately. A premium must be written down in accordance with the relevant accounting standards.

Merger accounting

Where the consideration for an acquisition is the issue of shares in the purchaser, the basic treatment should be to set up a share premium account for the amount by which the fair value exceeds the nominal value of the shares issued. Significant sums can thus be frozen in reserves which cannot be distributed. Merger accounting was initially developed to release pre-acquisition profits as distributable reserves in cases where the companies joining forces were of similar size. By this method the acquired company's shares were shown at the nominal value of the shares issued, goodwill did not arise and no change in the values of assets or liabilities was needed. The only increase in depreciation charge resulted from any change to standardise the accounting policies of the enlarged group. The consolidated profit and loss account included the full year's results for all the companies even though the merger occurred part way through the year. If the retained profits of the subsidiary on acquisition were paid to the new holding company as a dividend, this formed part of the distributable reserves.

Merger accounting lent itself to even more abuse than acquisition accounting. The case of *Shearer* v. *Bercain Limited* in 1980 first gave legal status to concerns about the position on distributable reserves and led to significant restrictions on the use of merger accounting in the Companies Act 1981. The method has fallen into disrepute. FRS 6 now restricts it for use for mergers in accounting periods starting on or after 23 December 1994 to the rare cases that cannot be properly be viewed as a takeover of one company by another. This standard sets out five criteria which must be satisfied if the combination is to be treated as a merger:

1. neither party to the transaction acts as the acquirer or acquired;
2. all parties participate in setting the basis for the management structure of the combined entity;
3. the relative sizes of both entities should not be so different as to allow one entity to dominate the combination due to its size;
4. shareholders of both entities should not receive significant amounts of cash or non-equity consideration;
5. no minority interests in the combined entity are permitted.

FRS 6 also sets out disclosure requirements, for both acquisitions and mergers, to ensure that full explanation of the effect of the combination is disclosed in the financial statements.

Annual report requirements

The Companies Acts require that the directors' report states the principal activities of the company during the year and any significant changes in those activities in the year. Many takeovers will need to be set out in summary in the directors' report to comply with this requirement in section 234(2) of Companies Act 1985 as amended. Schedule 7, Part II of that Act sets out in detail the disclosures required by a company acquiring its own shares. If this has happened then the information necessary must be included. It must not be forgotten that subsidiary companies' activities may also have changed significantly as a result of a takeover or other corporate activity within the group. Thus the matter needs to be considered carefully by the board of each subsidiary before approving the relevant directors' report.

If a takeover or other significant corporate event takes place early in the financial year before the previous year's accounts have been approved, the details of any post-balance sheet events must be included. This refers to any event of significance which has taken place after the date of the balance sheet and before the date on which it is signed. If such a matter is pending, then very careful consideration of the wording of Schedule 7, Part I, section 6 of the Companies Act 1985 will be needed.

Post-takeover audit

Many companies have systems to check that purchases of fixed assets or major investment projects have lived up to expectations. After the project is complete or the asset has been in use for a couple of years the internal audit department dust off the original justification files and check the expectation against the outcome. There is no reason why this process should not be applied to the purchase of a company as well as to that of a machine or building.

The internal investigation is in the best position to get a true comparison and to see how far the results differed from the expectation and in what direction. Acquisitions should be reviewed using the same techniques as were used in the original justification. Significant differences in outcome may cast light on the limitations of the techniques or of the way in which they were used, which will be of use in making future assessments. Where the results are largely favourable, then a cynical look at the original justification and at those who stood to benefit from its greater than expected success may be called for. In these days of performance targets and performance-based pay even natural optimists may become pessimists when making forecasts for which they will be held financially accountable.

The review should cover all aspects of the acquisition, unquantifiable as well as measurable. It should consider market share and other criteria as well as basic financial outcomes. The review is best discussed in the forum which would take the decision based on the justification. In the case of a major acquisition this will be by the board itself. At the very least, the decision-making body should check that the review has taken place and receive a summary of its key findings. In many cases the lessons do not need to be driven home but have been learnt in the course of the operation. None the less a review is valuable in providing a checklist on which to base cynical questions when considering the next similar proposal.

Operational gains from takeovers

I have suggested that the internal reviewers are in the best position to analyse the success or otherwise of a takeover. This has not stopped academics being fascinated by takeovers as a research field. The need to use information in the public domain to include a wide range of examples in this research has resulted in the majority of such investigations considering stock market returns. Franks and Harris in 1989 considered a sample of around 1,800 takeovers in the United Kingdom from 1955 to 1985. This analysis suggests that over the period of the takeover, on average, the shareholders of acquiring firms make zero or modest gains from the takeovers whereas the shareholders of the acquired firms gain in the region of 25 per cent to 30 per cent of the value of the acquired firm prior to the bid. Similar results have been reported in the United States. This would suggest that takeovers are not necessarily the result of managers pursuing their own self-interest without regard to the shareholders, but the results raise queries about the distribution of any benefits between the respective shareholders of the purchaser and the purchased.

A variety of papers suggest that the post-takeover performance of purchasers is poor in the sense that their stock market returns are abnormally low when measured by the use of some benchmark based on overall market performance. However, the results can vary with the definition of the benchmark for a normal stock market return and with the time period covered.

Market gains reflect a wide variety of factors. Benefits may arise from a concentration of ownership assisting the formation of cartels or from the effects of certain tax treatments.

Several researchers have sought to use accounting and analytical techniques to investigate whether shareholders' gains from takeovers and mergers arise as a consequence of improvements in operating activities. Results from work in the late 1970s and the 1980s found little evidence of operational gains, with the implication that most gains to shareholders result from financial or tax synergies or from reductions in capital expenditure requirements. This implication and the concerns over the possible abuses of the merger and acquisition accounting procedures raised questions. Did the conventional accruals accounting-based measures of performance used in these studies combined with the method of simply taking the difference between post- and pre-takeover performance as an indication of the change in performance caused by the takeover result in misleading conclusions?

Researchers at the University of Essex have recently published a study which uses cashflow data to examine post-takeover performance. The study constructs a pro forma 'consolidated' measure of the operating performance of purchaser and purchased for the five years before the year of takeover. It then compares this to the operating performance of the purchaser in the five years after the year of the takeover. Both measures take into account the average performance for the industries to which the companies belong. Operational gains are measured as the difference between post-takeover performance and a multiple of pre-takeover performance representing the level of performance that would have resulted in the absence of a takeover. In a sample of thirty-eight takeovers examined, operational gains were produced on average. Furthermore, the cashflow-based estimates of the operational gains from each takeover are associated with the market's *ex ante* assessments of total gains. It thus appears that the cashflow-based estimates capture phenomena of economic substance.

The results do not support the belief that changes in corporate control result from managers pursuing their own self-interest at the expense of shareholders. Rather, they support the proposition that the market for corporate control provides a disciplinary mechanism, which works in shareholders' interests.

Thus, the findings support the view that the market for corporate control:
(i) exists to promote competition between management teams for the use of resources and, as such, acts as an incentive mechanism to promote efficiency of many different kinds. This is particularly so with respect to operational efficiency; and
(ii) helps shareholders establish, and is set within a context in which shareholders have established, sufficient disciplinary controls over management to ensure that managers act in the interests of firms' owners.

The conclusion echoes US studies which have also used methodologies based on cashflow considerations. Cashflow data are more readily available than in the past as it can be derived from the disclosures required by FRS 1. The debate about the best methods to evaluate takeovers will no doubt continue. Without appropriate evaluation, reasons for making takeover bids remain subjective. Hence the need to review the justification in the light of events as well as before making the bid.

Appendix

Confidentiality undertaking for negotiations

Date:

Parties: (1) A Limited

            (2) B Limited

Whereas:

To explore the possibility [of buying B Limited ('the Company')]/[of buying the target business ('the Business')]/[of business opportunities of mutual interest] we may each need to disclose to the other proprietary information relating *inter alia* to our products, processes, research programmes and results, development and commercial activities. In order to protect our respective proprietary interests in the information we each disclose and in order to avoid misunderstandings, we wish to set out the terms and conditions on which the information is disclosed.

IT IS HEREBY AGREED:

1. that no announcement or disclosure of our interest in the Company/ Business/our mutual cooperation will be made by either party or on behalf of either party without the prior written consent from the other party.
2. that in this agreement the term 'Confidential Information' shall mean any information in any form emanating, directly or indirectly, from a party to this agreement and shall include any compilation of otherwise public information in a form not publicly known.
3. it is understood that the term 'Confidential Information' does not include:
    (i)   information which is publicly known at the time of its disclosure;
    (ii)   information which, after disclosure to the recipient, has become publicly known other than through breach of this agreement;
    (iii) information which the recipient can show was known to it prior to the disclosure by the other party;

     (iv) information which the recipient can show was developed indepen-
dently by a member of its staff who was not aware of the content of
the information disclosed by the other party;

     (v)   information which the recipient can show was made available to it
by a third party who had the right to do so and has not imposed on
the recipient any obligation of confidentiality or restricted use in
respect thereof.

4.   Each party agrees that it will not at any time disclose to any third party
any Confidential Information which it receives from the other and it shall
use the Confidential Information only for the purposes of considering and
evaluating [the purchase of the Company]/[the purchase of the Business]/
[the business opportunities of mutual interest] under discussion between
the parties.

5.   The distribution by each party of Confidential Information will be limited
to those of its employees and professional advisers involved with the
matter and each such employee and professional adviser shall be notified
of the terms of this undertaking. Each party shall use its best endeavours
to ensure that they abide by these obligations and shall be fully responsible
for any unauthorised disclosure or use of the Confidential Information by
its officers and employees.

6.   Any documents, printed or written or electronic material, designs,
drawings, models, samples, computer software or other tangible items
supplied by one party to the other in the course of their discussions of this
matter shall be returned promptly at the request of the party which
supplied them together with any copies thereof.

7.   This agreement shall automatically terminate if the parties enter into a
further agreement in connection with the subject matter of these
preliminary discussions which contains provisions dealing with the use and
disclosure of Confidential Information.

8.   In the event that discussions terminate without any further agreement
being entered into in connection with this matter then each party shall
return promptly to the other the Confidential Information and any
documents, printed or written or electronic material, designs, drawings,
models, samples, computer software or other tangible items supplied by
one party to the other in the course of their discussions of this matter
together with any copies thereof. The termination of discussions shall not
release either party from the obligations under paragraphs 4 or 5 above.

9.   It is recognised that:

     (i)   the furnishing of Confidential Information will not constitute an offer
by either party, nor the basis of any contract nor a representation
which may be relied upon by the other party;

     (ii) neither party nor their advisers accept responsibility for, nor make
or will make, any representation (express or implied) with respect to
the accuracy or completeness of the Confidential Information and

(iii) each party will be required in any further agreement concerning this matter to acknowledge that it has not relied on or been induced to enter into such agreement by the Confidential Information, or by any representation or warranty other than any expressly set out in such agreement.

10. This agreement shall be subject to English law and all disputes arising in connection herewith shall be submitted to the non-exclusive jurisdiction of the English courts. This agreement shall take effect on the date set out on the first page of this agreement.

In witness whereof the duly authorised representatives of the parties have executed this agreement in duplicate originals.

Signed	Signed
for and on behalf of	for and on behalf of
A Limited	B Limited
Position	Position
date	date

Section 212 application

Dear Sirs

We require you pursuant to section 212 of the Companies Act 1985 to provide us in writing within _____ days of the date of this letter the following information concerning your interest (within the meaning of sections 203–205 and section 208 of the Act) in our _____ shares:

(a) the number of shares in which you have an interest;

(b) the nature of your interest in these shares;

(c) the date(s) upon which you acquired your interest;

(d) the full names and addresses of each person (including investment managers) who also has an interest in these shares, together with particulars of the nature of each interest and the number of shares in which each person had an interest;

(e) [the number of shares in which you have had an interest at any time during the past three years;

(f) if you have disposed of any of these shares please specify the date(s) and the number of shares for each disposal; and to the best of your knowledge the identity of the person who held the beneficial interest immediately after your interest ceased;]

(g) [full details of any agreement or arrangement known to you relating to the exercise of any voting rights (including those covered by section 204 of the Companies Act 1985) applying to the shares in which you have or had an interest together with the names and addresses of each party to the agreement or arrangement.]

Yours faithfully

Minute appointing committee

Before any announcement

It was resolved that a committee of the board of directors be constituted to consist of any two directors of the company and to be authorised and appointed to attend to all matters arising in relation to the Offer including agreeing any changes to the Press Announcement, [other specified agreements] and any other relevant agreements and generally attending to, agreeing and settling all documentation and matters arising and any one member of such committee is authorised or empowered to sign for and on behalf of the company any such documents approved by the committee or the board.

After announcement and before document despatch

It was resolved that a committee of the board of directors be constituted to consist of any two directors of the company and to be authorised and appointed to attend to all matters arising in relation to the Offer including agreeing any changes to the Press Announcement, Offer Document, Form of Acceptance, Circular, Form of Proxy or any other documents referred to in these minutes and any other relevant documents and generally attending to, agreeing and settling all documentation and matters arising.

Preamble to committee minute

The chairman referred to the appointment of the committee pursuant to a resolution of the board on [date]. The committee was empowered to do all things considered by them to be necessary in connection with or arising out of the Offer for/by _____ and generally to exercise all the powers of the board as they deem necessary or expedient for that purpose. It was noted that the committee was duly constituted and quorate.

Board resolution to allow a [finance] director to complete bank facility documentation

It was resolved that:
the execution, delivery and performance by the company of the Facility Agreement and the Fee Letter and the terms thereof be approved;

the execution, delivery and performance by the company of any ancillary document, notice, certificate, waiver, amendment or other document (each an 'Ancillary Document') which may be required in connection with the Facility Agreement and the Fee Letter or otherwise be approved;

any director of the company be authorised to execute the Facility Agreement and the Fee Letter on behalf of the company substantially in the form produced to the meeting subject to such amendments being made thereto as (s)he may agree and so that his/her signature thereon shall be conclusive evidence of his/her agreement to any such amendments;

any director or the secretary of the company (each being an 'Authorised Signatory') be authorised to do all such acts and things and to execute and deliver all Ancillary Documents which may be required and to carry into effect the purposes of the foregoing resolutions and if any Ancillary Document needs to be executed as a deed that the same be executed under the common seal of the company or executed as a deed by any two Authorised Signatories in accordance with Section 36A (4) of the Companies Act 1985 subject to any amendments being made to such Ancillary Document(s) as the persons signing such document(s) may agree and so that his/her/their signatures thereon shall be conclusive evidence of his/her/their agreement to any such amendment;

the execution of any document referred to above by any person authorised to execute the same shall be conclusive evidence of the due authorisation by the company of the execution of such document.

Note: Earlier the minutes must define Facility Agreement, Fee Letter and Authorised Signatories.

List of documents for an offer

Assumes offer by a listed company (bidder) for another listed company (target) which is classified as Super Class 1.

Administrative documents

List of parties
Outline timetable
List of documents

Documents to be sent to target's shareholders

Summary of offer terms
Offer document
Listing particulars
Form of acceptance and transfer
Reply paid envelope

Section 429 notices and statutory declaration
Consideration cheques
Share certificates or other securities title documents
Proposals to option holders
Reminder letter

Documents to be sent to bidder's shareholders

Super Class 1 circular, including notice of extraordinary general meeting
Offer document (for information only)
Listing particulars
Form of proxy
Reply paid envelopes

Press releases

Announcing the terms of the offer
Announcing posting
Announcing result of bidder's extraordinary general meeting
Announcing that offer is unconditional in all respects
Announcing the level of acceptances at the first closing date
Announcing despatch of consideration/documents of title
Announcing despatch of s 429 notices

Legal matters

(i) *Bidder*
    Board minutes appointing committee to deal with matters arising
    Board minutes:
        to approve purchase of target in principle
        to approve offer terms
        to authorise press releases
        to approve documentation sent to bidder's and target's shareholders
        to approve working capital statement
        to approve indebtedness statement
        to approve application for listing
        to allot any consideration in shares
        to convene extraordinary general meeting
        to approve OFT submission
        to approve estimate of expenses
    Responsibility statements from all directors
    Powers of attorney
    Minutes of extraordinary general meeting

(ii) *Target*

    Board minutes appointing committee to deal with matters arising

    Board minutes:

        to approve press releases

        to recommend offer

    Powers of attorney

(iii) *General*

    Documents available for inspection

    Verification notes

    Irrevocable undertakings

    Proposals *re* options

Accounting matters

    Indebtedness statements

    Bank certificates supporting borrowings

    Bank facility letters

    Letter from accountants to bidder and bank/target and its bank on indebtedness

    Working capital report for enlarged group

    Letter from accountants to company and bank on adequacy of working capital for enlarged group

    Pro-forma statement of net assets for enlarged group

    Pro-forma indebtedness statement for enlarged group

    Tax effects letter and tax clearance application (if applicable)

    Comfort letter on financial information

Application for listing

    Stock Exchange approval for listing particulars

    Stock Exchange agreement to deal in the new shares/securities

    Application by sponsoring broker for admission to listing

    Six copies of listing particulars and all other documents sent to bidder's and target's shareholders

    Stock Exchange form for admission to listing

    Derogation letter to the Stock Exchange

    Certified copies of relevant board and other resolutions and other miscellaneous documents

    Listing fee

Miscellaneous

    Labels for bidder's shareholders and option holders

    Labels for target's shareholders

Labels for target's option holders
Estimate of expenses
List of major shareholders in bidder
List of major shareholders in target
List of key analysts, fund managers and journalists
Letter from brokers confirming share prices in offer document
Definitive share certificate (if new class of shares)
Article defining new class of shares (if any)
Definitive document of title (if new class of security)
Instrument constituting new class of security (if any)
Letters confirming valuations of new shares and/or securities
Advertisements
Takeover Panel fee
OFT submission
Letters to Panel *re* meetings
Block transfers
Section 198 notification
Letter to target's staff
Receiving agent's certificate
Receiving bank agreement

Documents for display

Memorandum and Articles of Association of bidder and target
Material contracts
Audited financial statements for the preceding two years for bidder and
    target and any subsequent interim statements
Consents and opinions
Any instrument constituting a security which forms part of the consideration
    for the offer
Directors' service contracts for directors of each company
Rules of share option schemes of each company
Irrevocable undertaking/share purchase agreement
Offer document
Super Class 1 circular including notice of extraordinary general meeting
Listing particulars

Timetable for an offer

Assumes offer by a listed company (bidder or company) for another listed
company (target) which is classified as Super Class 1.

Offer for Target Group PLC   Outline Offer Timetable

Date 19xx/yy	Task/event	Responsibility
Monday, 6 Dec (A–12) (D–37)	Completion of valuation of target and synergies	Company/accountants
	Start working capital review	Company/accountants
	Accounting and legal due diligence checklist prepared	Company/bank/accountants/solicitors
	Update meeting	All parties
Wednesday, 8 Dec (A–8) (D–33)	Finalise model of acquisition effects on company and financial structuring	Bank/company
	Drafting meeting on press release	All parties
Thursday, 9 Dec (A–7) (D–32)	Final draft of press release available	Bank/company
	Tactics finalised	All parties
	Board meeting to seek approval to approach target	Company
Friday, 10 Dec (A–6) (D–31)	Approach made to target	Company
Monday, 13 Dec (A–3) (D–28)	9.00 am Meeting to finalise terms of offer	All parties
	Announcement of approach	Target
	Start work on OFT submission	Company/solicitors
	Meetings with key shareholders in target	Target/brokers
	Draft irrevocable undertakings reviewed and distributed	Solicitors
	2.00 pm drafting meeting to discuss contents of: (a) presentation (b) offer press release (c) contents of target's shareholders' summary of offer terms	All parties
Tuesday, 14 Dec (A–2) (D–27)	Finalisation of press release	Bank/company/solicitors
	Verification of press release	Company/solicitors
	Form of irrevocable undertakings agreed	
	Rehearsal of presentation	Company/bank/brokers

Date 19xx/yy	Task/event	Responsibility
	List of parties, list of documents and timetable finalised and circulated	Bank
	Meeting to discuss working capital	Company/bank/accountants
Wednesday, 15 Dec (A–1) (D–26)	9.00 am pre-completion meeting	Company/target/banks
	Collection of signed irrevocable undertakings	Company/brokers
	5.00 pm bidder and target board meetings to: approve purchase of target approve offer terms approve press release approve target's shareholders' summary	Company/target
	Complete work on combined working capital review	Accountants
	Irrevocable undertakings held in escrow	Solicitors
	Presentation finalised	Company/bank/PR
	Press announcement printed	Bank
Thursday, 16 Dec (A) (D–25)	**DAY OF ANNOUNCEMENT OF PROPOSED OFFER**	
	8.00 am Announcement of firm intention to make an offer to the Stock Exchange	Company/bank/brokers
	Release of irrevocable undertakings from escrow	Solicitors
	Investor/analysts/press presentations	Company/target
	Printers' quotes for circular/listing particulars/offer document obtained	Bank
	Estimate of expenses prepared	Bank
	COMPANY INDEBTEDNESS DATE	
	TARGET INDEBTEDNESS DATE	
Friday, 17 Dec	Summary of offer terms posted to target's shareholders	Target
	Further PR as needed	Company/PR
	Printers appointed	Company/bank

Date 19xx/yy	Task/event	Responsibility
	First drafts of circular/listing particulars/offer document and form of acceptance to printer	Bank
	Work commences on formal working capital report	Accountants
	Formal letter of instruction to accountants	Bank
Monday, 20 Dec	Indebtedness review starts	Accountants
(A+4) (D–21)	First proof of documents circulated	Bank
Tuesday, 21 Dec (A+5) (D–20)	9.00 am drafting meeting	All parties
Wednesday, 22 Dec	Second proof of documents circulated	Printers
(A+6) (D–19)	Circular/listing particulars/offer document submitted to the Stock Exchange	Brokers
Thursday, 23 Dec (A+7) (D–19)	9.00 am drafting meeting	All parties
Friday, 24 Dec (A+8) (D–17)	Holiday proof of documents circulated	Printers
	Verification notes circulated	Solicitors
	Draft working capital and indebtedness statements available	Accountants
Saturday, 25 Dec (A+9) (D–16)	CHRISTMAS DAY	
Sunday, 26 Dec (A+10) (D–15)	BOXING DAY	
Monday, 27 Dec (A+11) (D–14)	BANK HOLIDAY	
Tuesday, 28 Dec (A+12) (D–13)	BANK HOLIDAY	
Thursday, 30 Dec (A+13) (D–12)	9.00 am progress meeting to discuss: working capital indebtedness status of documents	All parties
Saturday, 1 Jan (A+16) (D–9)	NEW YEAR'S DAY	
Monday, 3 Jan (A+17) (D–7)	BANK HOLIDAY	

Date 19xx/yy	Task/event	Responsibility
Wednesday, 5 Jan (A+20) (D–5)	9.00 am final drafting and verification meeting	All parties
	Working capital report and indebtedness statements finalised	Accountants
	Draft comfort letter and consent letters available	Accountants/bank
	Target shareholder labels to be submitted to printers	Target registrars
	Company shareholder labels to be submitted to printers	Registrars
Thursday, 6 Jan (A+21) (D–4)	Information on shareholdings/ dealings in bidder/target by directors and persons giving irrevocable undertakings finalised	Company/solicitors
	Verification complete	Company/solicitors
Friday, 7 Jan (A+22) (D–3)	Bidder and target board meetings to:	Company/target/ solicitors
	approve offer document	
	approve listing particulars	
	approve form of acceptance	
	approve circular	
	convene extraordinary general meeting	
	approve notice of and proxy card for the extraordinary general meeting	
	approve working capital forecast and indebtedness statement	
	approve estimate of expenses	
	approve despatch of documents	
	approve application for listing	
	Stock Exchange to agree to stamp circular	Brokers
	All documents into escrow	Solicitors
	Opinion and consent letters signed	
Saturday/Sunday, 8/9 Jan (A+23) (A+24) (D–2) (D–1)	Bulk print documents	Printers

Date 19xx/yy	Task/event	Responsibility
Monday, 10 Jan (A+25)(D)	**POSTING DAY**	
	Release documents from escrow	Solicitors
	Post offer documents, forms of acceptance and listing particulars to target's shareholders	Bank/company
	Post Super Class 1 circular, listing particulars, notice of extraordinary meeting, proxy card and offer document (for information only) to bidder's shareholders	Bank/company
	File documents with Registrar of Companies	Company/solicitors
	Deliver copies of documents to Company Announcements Office	Company/solicitors
	Lodge documents and Panel fee with Panel	Bank
	Lodge documents with Stock Exchange	Brokers
	Submit working capital letter and indebtedness statement to the Stock Exchange	Brokers
	Deliver OFT submission	Company/solicitors
	Announce posting of documents	Bank/company
Friday, 14 Jan (D+3)	Initial application to the Stock Exchange for admission to listing for new securities	Brokers
	Irrevocable acceptors to have accepted offer by 3.00 pm	Vendors
Wednesday, 19 Jan (D+9)	The Stock Exchange Committee hearing on the application for new securities to be admitted to the Official List	Brokers
Monday, 31 Jan (D+21)	Last date for receipt of proxies for extraordinary general meeting	
	First closing date of offer	
	Written confirmation of the number of acceptances received under the offer	Receiving bank

Date 19xx/yy	*Task/event*	*Responsibility*
	OFT indicates whether the offer will be referred to MMC	
Tuesday, 1 Feb (D+22)	Announce level of offer acceptance by 9.00 am and extend offer	Bank
Wednesday, 2 Feb (D+23)	Extraordinary general meeting (first day offer can be declared unconditional in all respects)	Company
Friday, 18 Feb (D+39)	Last date for announcement of significant financial information by target	
Monday, 21 Feb (D+42)	First date when target's shareholders have right of withdrawal if offer has not become unconditional as to acceptances	
Wednesday, 23 Feb (D+44)	If offer declared fully unconditional on D+23, consideration paid to accepting target shareholders	
Friday, 25 Feb (D+46)	Last date for revision and despatch of offer (including announcement of significant financial information by the bidder)	
Friday, 11 Mar (D+60)	Last date for declaring offer unconditional as to acceptances	
Friday, 1 Apr (D+81)	Last date for satisfaction of any other conditions and for offer to be declared fully unconditional (if acceptance conditions fulfilled on D+60)	
Friday, 22 Apr (D+102)	Last date for payment of consideration (if offer not fully unconditional until D+81)	
Thereafter	Despatch section 429 Notice within 2 months of acquiring 90 per cent	

Timetable for the back end

Offer for Target Group PLC

3 May 19xx	First day through 90 per cent
7 May 19xx	Offer declared wholly unconditional
8 May 19xx	Dealings in new securities commence
22 May 19xx	Despatch of section 429 notice to shareholders who have not accepted the Offer
28 May 19xx	Consideration despatched to accepting shareholders (as at 7 May)
25 June 19xx	Bidder gives 14 days' notice of closure of the Offer
3 July 19xx	Offer closes
	Section 429 closes
Thereafter	Notice to Stock Exchange that procedure completed
	Target shares are delisted

Agreement for consultant

This agreement is made on .... (date) .... between .... of .... ('the Company') and .... of .... ('the Consultant').

WHEREAS

the Consultant has agreed to provide services to the Company under the terms of a letter dated ....

It is hereby agreed that it will be a fundamental term of the contract between the Company and the Consultant that the Consultant observes the Secrecy Agreement set out below:

Secrecy agreement

1.   The Consultant understands that all information he/she may be given or may learn relating to the Company's business and/or that of its clients, including proprietary information and progress and results of researches, must be kept strictly secret. He/she will not directly or indirectly divulge or communicate the same to any person, firm or company either during the course of the above-mentioned contract for services or at any time after its termination unless under compulsion of the law or with the express authorisation in writing of the Company so to do.

2.   The Consultant agrees he/she will not use or take advantage in his/her private capacity of any such information or put into operation or take

advantage of any invention or process or technology of which he/she shall obtain knowledge in the course of the contract for services.

3.   The whole of the copyrights and rights in the nature of copyright throughout the world for the whole term in each country, and all extensions and renewals thereof in all material which is prepared by the Consultant and all products, discoveries, inventions, designs or other results of the services provided by the Consultant in respect of any work carried out by him/her under this agreement shall belong to the Company absolutely. The Consultant shall, at the Company's request and expense, execute such assignments or other documents (whether in favour of the Company or otherwise as it may direct) and do all such acts and things as the Company may direct to give effect hereto.

4.   The Consultant will not publish any information or articles connected with his/her work with the Company without the prior written consent of the Company.

5.   The Consultant is required to comply with the Company guidelines for the dissemination of price-sensitive information and to comply with the insider dealing rules during the course of the above-mentioned contract for services and for six months following its termination. The Consultant will deliver to the secretary of the Company signed copies of the guidelines for the dissemination of price-sensitive information and of the insider dealing rules at the time of signing of this contract.

In witness whereof the parties hereto have executed this agreement in duplicate originals the day and year first above written.

Signed as a deed by the Company by
.... Director
.... Director/Secretary

Signed as a deed by
....
in the presence of
....
....
....

Script for extraordinary general meeting

Company PLC

Extraordinary general meeting of the company to be held at ..... on ..... at [3.00 pm].

Procedure

Chairman Ladies and gentlemen it is just past [3.00 pm] and I would like to commence this extraordinary general meeting of Company PLC.

For your information, the quorum for a general meeting of the members shall be [three] members present in person. The registrars have confirmed that a quorum is present.
With your approval, I propose to take the notice convening the meeting as read.

(pause)

Statement explaining the reasons for the Special Resolution set out in the Notice of the Extraordinary General Meeting.

(pause)

The resolution will be formally proposed and seconded. We will then answer any questions relevant to the resolution. When any such questions have been answered, I will put the resolution to the vote. Only shareholders or their duly appointed representatives are entitled to vote.

Resolution: I now propose as a special resolution the resolution as set out in the notice convening the meeting and I will ask .... to second the resolution.

.... Mr Chairman, I am happy to second the resolution.

Chairman Thank you. Are there any questions relating to the resolution?

(Chairman deals with questions.)

I will now put the resolution to the meeting.

Those in favour?

Those against?

(A majority of 75 per cent of those present and voting is required to pass this resolution. If this is not achieved, see appendix.)

I declare the resolution carried.

Appendix for extraordinary general meeting

The resolution has not been carried on a show of hands. In my capacity as chairman, and in accordance with your company's Articles of Association, I straight away demand a poll and I shall ask the representative of the registrars to conduct that poll.

As I have mentioned, only shareholders or their duly appointed representatives are entitled to vote on the poll.

Will the representative of the registrars please distribute and collect the voting papers. If you require a voting paper, please raise your hand.

Will you please indicate by a cross on the paper whether you vote for or against the resolution.

Please also ensure that your name is clearly shown on the paper. Shareholders who have already given proxies and do not wish to alter their vote need not vote in person. Indeed, it will make the count of the vote simpler if those shareholders who have already sent in proxies abstain now from voting again in person.

You may be interested to know that proxies have been lodged either in favour of the resolution or at my discretion, or alternatively against the resolution as follows:

　　　　　　(Registrar's proxy certificate will be tabled)
　　　　　　(Distribution, completion and collection of voting papers)

Have all those entitled handed in their voting papers?

　　　　　　(Wait while the count is conducted.)

On declaring the result:

Ladies and gentlemen, I have now received from the registrars details of the poll. They are as follows:

Votes for the resolution ....
Votes against ....

I therefore declare the resolution carried.

Procedure where shareholder is to be silenced and removed

Chairman   Ladies and Gentlemen, I think we have had sufficient discussion on this matter and I propose that we now proceed with the business of the meeting.

I THEREFORE PUT TO THE MEETING THE PROPOSAL THAT WE NOW PROCEED WITH THE BUSINESS OF THE MEETING.

Those in favour, please raise their hands;
those against.
The resolution to proceed is therefore carried.

(The chairman then attempts to proceed with the business of the meeting. If the shareholder continues to interrupt:)

Chairman   Ladies and Gentlemen, I think we have all heard enough of this gentleman/this lady/these gentlemen/these people and I THEREFORE PUT TO THE MEETING THAT THIS SHAREHOLDER/THESE SHAREHOLDERS BE NO LONGER HEARD.

Chairman   Those in favour?

Those against?

This resolution is therefore carried. Thank you. Perhaps we can now get on with the business of the meeting.

(If the shareholder(s) continue(s) to speak, the chairman says:)

Chairman   A resolution has been proposed and passed that you be no longer heard. If, therefore, you do not sit down I must ask you to leave the meeting.

(If he/she/they refuse to leave, then:)

Chairman   I am afraid that I have no alternative but to suspend the proceedings of the meeting for a few minutes to give this gentleman/this lady/these gentlemen/these people an opportunity to leave the meeting.

(Pause to allow him/her/them to leave peacefully.)

(At this stage, shareholder(s) is/are assisted from the meeting by several persons with no more force than is reasonably necessary to ensure that he/she goes (they go) and remain(s) outside the meeting.)

(If disruption is such as to require a brief adjournment to restore order, the chairman should say:)

Chairman   It is quite impossible for this meeting to continue while this disruption is going on. In order to enable order to be restored, I adjourn this meeting for [15] minutes.

Chairman   Ladies and gentlemen, now that he/she/they has/have left the meeting, we can proceed to the unfinished business.
I must apologise to members and others here on their behalf for this disturbance. I am sure that this has been as much a trial to you as it has been to us.

The chairman then returns to the original script.

Glossary

ACT Advance Corporation Tax is paid by a company on the dividend distributed to shareholders within three months of the distribution. The ACT may usually be set against the gross amount of corporation tax due at the end of the year and surplus ACT may be carried forward or back. There are restrictions on the use of surplus ACT when the ownership or trade of a company changes. The shareholder obtains a tax credit for the ACT paid by the company.

Administrators An appointment under the Insolvency Act 1986 with powers similar to those normally conferred on a receiver.

AGM The annual general meeting of a company required to be held by section 366 of the Companies Act 1985.

Alternative Investment Market (AIM) A market for as wide a range of companies as possible regulated by the London Stock Exchange which opened during 1995.

Big Bang The changes in 1986 to the London Stock Exchange which included changes in ownership of member firms, transfer of voting rights from individuals to the firms and the abolition of minimum commissions.

Blue Book A colloquial name for the City Code on Takeovers and Mergers and The Rules Governing Substantial Acquisitions of Shares. Called for its blue A5 cover.

Bonus issue A capitalisation issue where new shares are allotted, fully paid, to existing holders pro rata to their holdings, for example one new share for every five shares held. A '1 for 1' issue would double the number of shares held by each holder but halve the share price and so is often used when the share price has become heavyweight.

Chinese walls An established arrangement whereby information known to persons involved in one part of a business is not available (directly or indirectly) to those involved in another part of the business and it is accepted that in each part of the business decisions are taken without reference to any interest which any other part of the business may have in the matter.

City Code The Code published and administered by the Panel on Takeovers and Mergers to ensure good business practice and fairness to the shareholders of publicly quoted companies.

Class meetings General meetings of holders of a particular class of security (usually other than ordinary shares) held in accordance with the rules laid down in the relevant Article of Association, trust deed or other instrument establishing the securities and the rights of their holders.

Class tests The classifications of takeovers used by the Stock Exchange to determine the level of disclosure and consultation with shareholders required. Covered in detail in Chapter 4.

Company Announcements Office The department of the London Stock Exchange which deals with announcements by companies regulated by the Exchange.

Continuing Obligations These are the obligations with which a listed company has to comply in order to enjoy the benefits of listing on the London Stock Exchange. There are similar though less onerous continuing obligations for those quoted on the Alternative Investment Market.

Convertible securities A convertible is a preference share or loan stock which may, at the holder's discretion, be exchanged on a given date each year for ordinary shares in the company.

CREST is the new settlement system for the UK equity industry. It is being built by the Bank of England to replace the existing Stock Exchange system.

Debt securities Forms of tradeable debt including debentures and loan stocks.

dti The Department of Trade and Industry was established in 1621 to identify 'the true causes of the decay of trade and scarcity of coyne'. It is the government department most closely concerned with the promotion and regulation of business and commerce.

Earn out An arrangement whereby the vendor remains with the business for a period and the consideration is paid over time and related to the continuing performance.

Earnings cap In 1989 tax relief on pension payments was capped so that high earners are limited in the extent to which relief can be claimed. It does not apply to those who started their current pensionable employment before 1989.

EGM An extraordinary general meeting of shareholders is the term used for any company general meeting other than the annual general meeting required to be held under section 366 of the Companies Act 1985.

Eurobonds   When an institution borrows money on the international money market in a currency which is not that of its home country, it is dealing in Eurocurrency. Eurobonds are bonds by which institutions can raise money on the Eurocurrency market.

Extraordinary resolution   A resolution which has been passed by a majority of not less than three-fourths of such members entitled to vote as are present in person or by proxy at a general meeting. Notice specifying the intention to propose the resolution as an extraordinary resolution must have been given. The requirements are set out in section 378 of the Companies Act 1985.

Financial assistance   Section 151 of the Companies Act 1985 prohibits a company from giving financial assistance for the purchase of its own shares. This includes assistance by way of a gift, a loan or a guarantee.

Flotation   A term commonly used for the initial issue or sale of shares to obtain a quotation on a recognised market.

FRS   Financial Reporting Standard; a series of standards issued by the Accounting Standards Board generally relating to the presentation of the accounts.

Listing Rules   The regulations governing admission to listing and the Continuing Obligations of issuers made by the Stock Exchange as empowered by Part IV of the Financial Services Act 1986.

Management buy-out   The purchase of a company from its existing share-holders by the senior management, often with the assistance of venture capitalists.

Management buy-in   The purchase of a company by new shareholders who intend to become its active management, often backed by venture capitalists.

Model Code   This code restricts the dealings in a listed company's shares to avoid directors placing themselves in a position where they could be suspected of taking advantage of price-sensitive information. A listed company must ensure compliance by its directors, employees who are privy to price-sensitive information and persons connected with the directors and those employees.

Novation   is, in effect, a form of assignment in which, by the consent of all parties, a new contract is substituted for an existing contract. Usually, but not necessarily, a new person becomes party to the new contract and some person who was party to the old contract is discharged from further liability.

Options   An option gives the holder the right but not the obligation to deal in an underlying asset at a fixed exercise or strike price between the date the option is acquired and a specified date in the future. A call option gives the right to buy; a put option gives the right to sell.

Ordinary resolution   This is a resolution passed by a simple majority of those voting. It is used for all matters not requiring an extraordinary or special resolution under the Companies Acts or the Articles of Association of the company.

Placing   An arrangement whereby a company offers its shares directly to the investing institutions rather than offer them to the general public.

Poison pill   The issue of special shares carrying extra voting or dividend rights which are triggered when a hostile bid is made or else a clause in the Articles of Association demanding exceptional voting requirements for the implementation of mergers.

Preference shares   usually carry preferential rights in relation to dividends but there may be any kind of preference so long as each preference is clearly defined in the relevant article.

Private company   A company which is not a public company as defined by section 1 of the Companies Act 1985.

Public company   A company which is a public company must be designated as such by the letters PLC or by public limited company (or the Welsh equivalents) in its name, having a minimum issued share capital (currently £50,000) and shares paid up to the extent of 25 per cent at least.

Receiver   correctly an administrative receiver is the insolvency practitioner appointed to manage a company's property by or on behalf of the holders of any debentures or other loans secured by a charge.

Redeemable securities   Shares which can be redeemed, that is bought back and cancelled by the company, under the terms of its Articles and of sections 159–161 of the Companies Act 1985.

Rights issue   A means by which a company raises money through the issue of shares to investors at a discount to the prevailing market price and in proportion to their existing holdings.

SARs   The rules governing substantial acquisitions of shares in quoted companies which are administered by the Takeover Panel and set out in the second part of the Blue Book (*q.v.*).

Scrip issue   Another name for a bonus or capitalisation issue.

Self-administered pension scheme   This scheme is one where the trustees are responsible for the overall investment strategy and can decide who will administer the scheme.

Self-investment (pensions)   There are regulations which restrict the extent to which occupational pension schemes may invest in the sponsoring company or any other company associated or connected with it.

SEPON SEPON Limited (Stock Exchange Pool Nominees) has a single undesignated shareholding account in the register of every company traded through the TALISMAN transaction system. Under this system all sold stock is transferred to SEPON Limited and purchasers receive their stock by transfer out of the SEPON Ltd account, which is a pool of all shares in the course of settlement.

SERPS The State Earnings Related Pension Scheme which provides an earnings-related pension in addition to the basic state pension.

Special resolution A resolution which has been passed in the manner required for the passing of an extraordinary resolution at a general meeting but not less than 21 days' notice specifying the intention to propose the resolution as a special resolution must have been given; see sections 378 and 379 of the Companies Act 1985.

Sponsor An issuer must appoint or have in place a sponsor when it makes an application for listing requiring the production of listing particulars, when required to do so by the Stock Exchange following a breach of the Listing Rules or when the listing rules require a report from a sponsor, such as the profit forecast in a Super Class 1 circular.

Stock Exchange The International Stock Exchange of the United Kingdom and the Republic of Ireland Limited commonly known as the London Stock Exchange.

Takeover Code The City Code published and administered by the Panel on Takeovers and Mergers to ensure good business practice and fairness to the shareholders of publicly quoted companies.

Vendor placing A vendor placing occurs where the purchaser issues new shares to the seller but arranges with an institution for the immediate resale of such shares in the market and guarantees in the sale and purchase agreement that the sale of the shares will yield the seller the right amount of consideration.

Vendor rights scheme also known as a vendor placing with clawback. Similar to a vendor placing but the merchant bank, acting as broker, will first offer the shares to the bidder's existing shareholders in proportion to their existing shareholdings to avoid the dilution of their interest.

Warrants are options issued by the company which are tradeable and usually quoted. These are normally used as a sweetener in conjunction with the issue of other securities and give the right to subscribe for shares in the company at a fixed price for a fixed period in the future or, occasionally, in perpetuity.

Warranty A warranty is an assurance by the vendor that a particular state of affairs exists. Breach of warranty entitles the purchaser to claim damages which equal any amount reasonably foreseeable at the time of the contract as likely to flow from the breach.

Whitewash   The Whitewash guidance note in appendix to the City Code sets out the procedures to be followed if the Panel is asked to waive an obligation to make a general offer under rule 9 of the Code because a person or a group of persons acting in concert have acquired shares to an extent which would normally give rise to an obligation to make a general offer as a result of the issue of new securities as consideration for an acquisition or a cash injection or in fulfilment of obligations under an agreement to underwrite the issue of new securities.

Yellow Book   The Listing Rules of the London Stock Exchange.

Further reading

Ashe, M. and Counsell, L. (1993) *Insider Trading*, 2nd edition, Croydon: Tolley.

Button, M. and Walker, P. (eds.) (1993) *A Practitioner's Guide to the City Code on Takeovers and Mergers*, Woking: Westminster Management Consultants.

Button, M. and Walker, P. (eds.) (1994) *A Practitioner's Guide to the Stock Exchange Yellow Book*, Woking: Westminster Management Consultants.

Cohen, J. (1993) *The Highest Bidder*, London: Penguin Books.

Franks, J. and Harris, R. (1989) 'Shareholder wealth effects of corporate takeovers: the UK experience 1955–85', *Journal of Financial Economics*, vol. 23, pp. 225–49.

Mallin, C. A. (1995) *The Role of Institutional Investors in Corporate Governance*, London: Research Board of the Institute of Chartered Accountants in England & Wales.

Manson, S., Stark, A. W. and Thomas, H. M. (1994) *A Cash Flow Analysis of the Operational Gains from Takeovers*, London: Certified Accountants Educational Trust.

Nash, T. (ed.) (1994) *Director's Guide to Buying and Selling Private Companies*, London: Director Publications.

Nash, T. (ed.) (1993) *Director's Guide to Management Buy-outs*, London: Director Publications.

Rock, S. (ed.) (1990) *Director's Guide to Corporate Finance*, London: Director Publications.

Smith, T. (1992) *Accounting for Growth*, London: Century Business.

Stapley, N. (1994) *The Private Investor's Guide to the Stockmarket*, Leighton Buzzard: ProShare.

Walmsley, K. (compiler) (1995) *Company Secretarial Practice*, 24th supplement, Hemel Hempstead: ICSA Publishing.

(1993) *The City Code on Takeovers and Mergers and The Rules Governing Substantial Acquisitions of Shares*, 4th edition, London: The Panel on Takeovers and Mergers.

(1994) *Company Acquisitions Handbook*, 3rd edition, Croydon: Tolley.

(1994) *The Takeover Panel 1993–1994 Report*, London: The Panel on Takeovers and Mergers.

(1994) *The Listing Rules*, 4th amendment, London: The London Stock Exchange.

(1995) *National Association of Pension Funds Limited Annual Survey 1994*, London: NAPF.

The Company Secretary, vol. 4, no. 5, March 1995, London: The Institute of Chartered Secretaries and Administrators.

Statutes

Fair Trading Act 1973
Restrictive Trade Practices Act 1976
Unfair Contract Terms Act 1977
Employment Protection (Consolidation) Act 1978
Theft Act 1978
Competition Act 1980
Companies Act 1985
Companies Securities (Insider Dealing) Act 1985
Financial Services Act 1986
Companies Act 1989
Trade Union and Labour Relations (Consolidation) Act 1992
Criminal Justice Act 1993
Trade Union Reform and Employment Rights Act 1993

Index